Echoes from the Eastern Shore

Echoes from the Eastern Shore

Twelve Native American Chiefs and the Fight for the Atlantic Homelands

Vol. 1 Spirits Unbroken Series

By Ward McLendon
Unbound Press

Echoes from the Eastern Shore: Twelve Native American Chiefs and the Fight for the Atlantic Homelands (Vol. 1 Spirits Unbroken)

Ward McLendon

Practices, regulations, and technology may change; consult current sources and institutional policies.

References to real organizations, products, devices, or services are for identification only and do not imply endorsement or affiliation. Where research findings or statistics are cited, sources are provided in notes or references. Absence of a citation does not imply universal consensus.

ISBN Ebook: 978-1-971207-17-9

ISBN Paperback 978-1-971207-16-2

ISBN Hardcover 978-1-971207-15-5

About the Series: Spirits Unbroken is a multi-volume biographical history of Indigenous leadership in North America, organized by region and grounded in documented historical record.

Across centuries of invasion, displacement, war, treaty-making, and forced assimilation, Native nations did not vanish. They adapted, resisted, negotiated, rebuilt, and endured. This series tells that story through the lives of the chiefs, leaders, and women who carried responsibility for their people in moments of profound crisis.

Rather than presenting Native history as a single experience, Spirits Unbroken treats each nation as politically distinct, culturally specific, and historically situated. The volumes are organized geographically to reflect how land, environment, and colonial pressure shaped different forms of leadership and survival.

These biographies focus not only on warfare but also on diplomacy, law, spiritual authority, kinship, and cultural continuity. They examine how Indigenous leaders confronted expanding empires, internal division, broken treaties, forced removals, and the long consequences of contact—while still defending sovereignty, identity, and future generations.

The final volume centers Indigenous women, whose leadership was often exercised outside formal titles but was no less decisive—through governance, resistance, preservation of culture, and survival itself.

Spirits Unbroken is not a celebration of defeat nor a simplification of heroism. It is a record of endurance: of nations that refused erasure, and of leaders who acted under impossible constraints to keep their people alive.

Table of Contents

Dedication

To the people of the nations that were here before the coast had borders, and who remain after the borders were drawn.

"We are still here."

—   Crowfoot

Note on Terminology

The term Native American is used throughout this volume for clarity and consistency, as it remains widely recognized in the United States. Indigenous is also used where appropriate, particularly in broader or comparative contexts. Neither term is meant to suggest a single culture, identity, or experience.

The word chief is used as a general term for individuals who held recognized leadership authority within their societies. Indigenous nations used many titles—such as sachem, sagamore, headman, or confederacy leader—and leadership structures varied widely by region and period. When specific titles or political roles are known, they are identified in the text.

Tribal and national names reflect a mix of self-identifiers and historically documented English or French spellings, depending on available sources. In cases where multiple spellings exist, this volume uses the most widely accepted form while noting significant variations when relevant.

Geographic references use modern place names to help orient readers, even when those names did not exist at the time described. This is done solely for clarity and does not imply historical ownership or legitimacy.

Finally, this book recognizes that the Native nations discussed here continue to exist today. Their histories do not end with colonization, removal, or treaty-making. This volume focuses on a specific historical period, not the full scope of any people's past or present.

Preface

This volume is organized by geography because geography determined survival.

Along the Atlantic coast, Indigenous nations experienced colonization first—and longest. The pressures they faced were not uniform. Coastal trade networks, river systems, imperial rivalries, disease, and land hunger shaped each region differently.

The biographies in this book are not isolated life stories. Each chief profiled here serves as an entry point into a broader political and cultural landscape. Their leadership cannot be understood apart from the nations they represented, the alliances they navigated, or the colonial systems pressing against them. For that reason, each section combines individual biography with broader regional history.

Readers will encounter overlapping events, recurring confederacies, and familiar pressures across chapters. This is intentional. Colonization was not a series of isolated encounters but a continuous process unfolding across generations and regions.

This volume does not attempt to catalog every tribe or every leader of the Atlantic homelands. It focuses on twelve chiefs whose lives illuminate the broader struggle for land, sovereignty, and survival during the first centuries of sustained European invasion.

Introduction

The Atlantic coast was not a frontier waiting to be discovered. It was a homeland—densely inhabited, politically complex, and governed by nations with long-established systems of law, diplomacy, trade, and war. When Europeans arrived along its shores, they entered an existing world, not an empty one.

This volume examines that world through the lives of twelve Native American chiefs whose leadership shaped the earliest centuries of sustained contact along the Atlantic seaboard. Their stories span the Gulf of Maine, Southern New England, the Hudson River corridor, the Mid-Atlantic river systems, and the Chesapeake Tidewater. Together, they reveal how Indigenous nations confronted an invasion that unfolded unevenly yet relentlessly, pressing inland from the sea.

The period covered here is often framed in American history as a story of settlement and founding. From the Indigenous perspective, it was a period of escalating pressure—marked by epidemics that preceded colonization itself, followed by trade dependencies, territorial encroachment, warfare, forced treaties, and displacement.

These forces did not arrive all at once, nor did they affect every nation in the same way. Geography mattered, as did timing, alliances, internal divisions, and the strategies adopted by individual leaders.

Leadership in Indigenous societies was neither uniform nor absolute. Authority was shaped by kinship, council consensus, spiritual responsibility, and the ability to persuade rather than command. Chiefs had obligations to their people, not sovereign power over them. Decisions to fight, negotiate, relocate, or accommodate were constrained by factors beyond any one leader's control. Understanding those constraints is essential to understanding the choices recorded in colonial sources—and the silences where those sources fail.

Readers will encounter familiar events—alliances with European powers, cycles of trade and dependency, and wars labeled as "Indian" conflicts in colonial records. These labels obscure the fact that Indigenous nations rarely responded to a single empire alone. French, English, Dutch, and later American interests collided along the coast, and Native leaders navigated those rivalries with strategic intent. Some sought balance through diplomacy. Others chose resistance when accommodation failed. None operated in isolation.

The Atlantic homelands were also linked to powerful inland networks. The Haudenosaunee Confederacy, river-based nations such as the Lenape and Susquehannock, and interior peoples of Virginia shaped coastal outcomes even when they lived far from the sea. Trade routes, military alliances, and population movements tied the coast to the interior, and this volume treats these connections as central rather than peripheral.

Colonial records dominate the written archive for this period and pose inherent challenges. Many accounts were produced by missionaries, traders, or officials whose priorities distorted their observations. Indigenous voices often appear only indirectly, filtered through translation or recorded only when they intersected with colonial interests. Where possible, this volume draws on Indigenous oral histories, later tribal scholarship, and archaeological evidence to correct or complicate those records.

This book does not present its subjects as tragic inevitabilities or symbolic figures standing in for an entire people. They were political actors making decisions in real time, with incomplete information and limited options.

Some choices resulted in short-term survival at long-term cost. Others led to catastrophic loss. Judging those outcomes without understanding the conditions under which they were made risks repeating the moral simplifications of earlier histories.

The chapters that follow do not tell a single story of Native America. They tell many stories—of confederacies forged and fractured, of land defended and lost, of diplomacy attempted and betrayed, and of cultures adapting under pressure. What unites them is not defeat but endurance. Despite centuries of displacement and erasure, the nations discussed in this volume did not disappear. They persist.

Echoes from the Eastern Shores opens the Spirits Unbroken series because the Atlantic homelands were the first place where these pressures converged and the longest where they were sustained. The leaders profiled here confronted the initial shock of invasion and its generational aftermath. Their stories form the foundation for understanding what followed as colonization moved inland and westward.

This is neither the beginning nor the conclusion of Native history. It is the record of a turning point—when Indigenous nations along the Atlantic coast were forced to defend their homelands against forces that would reshape an entire continent, and when survival itself became an act of leadership.

Part I — Gulf of Maine and the Wabanaki World

Chapter 1 — A Coast in Motion

We don't inherit the earth from our ancestors, we borrow it from our children.

—Native American Proverb

The Atlantic Homelands

ON A LATE AUTUMN morning in 1620, Massasoit stood near the edge of the water and watched the sea.

The shoreline was quiet. The tide was moving out across the flats, leaving dark bands of kelp and wet sand that reflected the pale sky. The air carried the smell of salt and decaying leaves, the season already turning. For weeks, perhaps longer, his people had spoken of a ship anchored beyond the reach of the surf—a large, square-rigged vessel riding deeper in the water than the fishing boats that sometimes appeared along the coast.

This ship was different.

The Wampanoag were no strangers to Europeans. Long before this moment, they had traded with passing crews, watched ships come and go, and heard stories of failed settlements—outposts abandoned after hunger, sickness, or conflict made them untenable. Foreign visitors were not new. What was new was permanence.

The vessel offshore did not leave.

From a distance, Massasoit could see the signs: the careful anchoring, the small boats moving back and forth, and the deliberate pace of men who expected to stay. This was not a trading expedition or a fishing crew waiting for the weather to turn. This was a settlement in motion.

Illustration, English ship

The timing could not have been worse.

Only a few years earlier, sickness had swept through the coastal villages with devastating force. Entire communities had been emptied. Fields went untended. Councils lost elders whose authority had anchored political life for generations. The Wampanoag Confederacy—once strong, expansive, and secure—had been weakened at precisely the moment when its rivals were not. To the west and south, the Narragansett remained powerful. To the east and north, other nations watched closely as they recalculated the balance of power.

Massasoit understood what the ship represented. New people meant new pressures. They could become allies—or enemies.

He also understood that the moment demanded restraint. Strength alone would not determine what followed. Survival would depend on judgment.

For thousands of years before that ship appeared on the horizon, the peoples of this coast had lived in a world shaped by water, seasons, and negotiated boundaries. The land the English would soon call New England was not an untouched wilderness. It was a managed landscape, shaped by agriculture, controlled burns, fishing weirs, trade routes, and diplomacy.

It was not unoccupied.

They called it Wabanaki—Dawnland—the place where the sun rises first, where rivers run cold and fast from the interior and spread into bays thick with fish and fog. The people later gathered under the label Wabanaki Confederacy were not a single tribe but an alliance of neighboring nations—bound by marriage ties, trade routes, shared enemies, and the hard arithmetic of survival once Europeans arrived in force. In that world, identity was anchored to watersheds and seasons: the river you traveled, the coast you harvested, the portage you carried across when the ice broke, and the canoes you went back in.

The Wolastoqiyik, often called the Maliseet in older English sources, were the people of the Wolastoq, the "bright" or "shining" river Europeans renamed the Saint John. Their homeland was a long river corridor running

5

through today's New Brunswick into northern Maine, a place where power came from controlling movement: who could pass upriver, who could trade, who could be fed in winter, who could be warned in time.

To know the Wolastoqiyik is to picture birchbark canoes gliding along tributaries, villages tied to the rhythms of salmon and moose, and a politics shaped by proximity—Mi'kmaq to the east, Penobscot to the west, Passamaquoddy to the south—neighbors who could be allies one season and rivals the next, depending on what the French and English offered and demanded.

South of them, where the coastline breaks into coves and islands, and the water turns brackish, lived the Passamaquoddy—Peskotomuhkatiyik—a people whose center of gravity was the bay that still carries their name.

Their homeland straddled what would become the U.S.–Canada border, but their lives didn't: the sea and the shore were the real map. Passamaquoddy communities were sustained by marine abundance and by the certainty that fishing places—villages like Sipayik (Pleasant Point)—were not merely "locations" but living archives, where families returned year after year to work, feast, argue, decide, and remember. In early contact history, that coastal position mattered. It put them in the path of fishing fleets and traders early on and made them essential brokers in the shifting diplomacy of the Northeast.

The Abenaki—Wôbanaki in their own language—formed another crucial span of the Dawnland, stretching across river valleys and interior routes that linked the Gulf of

Maine to the St. Lawrence. Here, the usual shorthand—Eastern Abenaki and Western Abenaki—is less about two separate "tribes" than about language and geography: Eastern Abenaki communities were concentrated more in what is now Maine, while Western Abenaki communities were centered more in Quebec, Vermont, and New Hampshire, tied into the north–south corridors of the Champlain and Connecticut systems.

In Wabanaki politics, the Abenaki mattered because they occupied the region's connective tissue—routes armies used, routes refugees fled along, and routes trade followed—so they were often the ones forced to decide, again and again, whether a new alliance offered protection or only postponed the next blow

The Wampanoag Confederacy governed a broad territory of coastal plains, rivers, and woodlands. Villages shifted with the seasons. Cornfields were planted and harvested with precision. Fishing runs were anticipated and regulated. Authority rested not in a single ruler but in networks of sachems and councils, bound by kinship, obligation, and custom. Diplomacy was essential, especially as European rivalries between France and England began to disrupt existing Indigenous power balances.

This was not a static society. It adapted constantly to climate, internal rivalry, and external pressure. Trade connected coastal peoples with those living inland. News traveled faster than outsiders could grasp. Decisions were weighed collectively, with memory stretching back generations. These were not scattered villages operating in isolation. They were nations—some small, some expansive—refined over generations.

Across North America, Indigenous nations had built similarly complex worlds. From the Gulf of Maine to the Chesapeake, from the Great Lakes to the plains beyond, societies rose and fell, confederacies formed and fractured, and systems of governance evolved long before Europeans began keeping records. Many Indigenous societies were organized around rivers and shorelines that functioned as transportation corridors, food sources, and defensive boundaries. Hunting territories and sacred spaces were regulated through custom and negotiation.

Leadership was situational and relational, not absolute. Authority flowed from consensus, lineage, spiritual responsibility, and the ability to persuade rather than command. These were not accidental cultures but the result of millennia of lived experience.

The arrival of Europeans did not introduce history to the continent. It introduced disruption.

Disease arrived first, moving faster than settlers, killing without negotiation or warning. Then came trade, which brought tools and weapons alongside dependency. Then came settlements—fenced, fortified, permanent. What had once been occasional contact hardened into occupation.

Massasoit had no way of knowing how far this process would go. No one did. What he could see, standing on the shore, was that the old balance had already begun to shift. The presence offshore posed a question to his people and to the region itself: resist, accommodate, or attempt something in between?

That decision would shape who lived, who ruled, and who remained.

In the years that followed, Massasoit would choose accommodation—not out of trust or naïveté, but calculation. He would attempt to fold the newcomers into an existing political world, to make them one power among many rather than a force apart. For a time, it would work.

Illustration of Atlantic Coast

But the ship on the horizon marked the beginning of a new phase in the history of the Atlantic homelands—one in which the choices available to Indigenous leaders narrowed with each passing decade, and in which survival itself became a form of resistance.

This book begins there, at the edge of the water, before outcomes were certain and before American history had a name. It is the story of the leaders who faced that horizon first, and of the nations who fought—by diplomacy, by war, and by endurance—to remain on the land they had always called home.

Their world did not disappear with contact. It collided with it.

The Many Nations

The Hudson Valley and Long Island formed another political crossroads. Here, numerous closely related communities governed distinct territories while navigating the influence of larger inland powers—most notably the Haudenosaunee Confederacy. The Five (later Six) Nations wielded enormous influence over trade, warfare, and diplomacy across the Northeast, shaping outcomes along the coast even though their villages lay far inland.

South of New England, the Lenape homelands along the Delaware River basin sustained a sophisticated river-based society that linked the Atlantic coast to the interior. Lenape communities regulated access to land and waterways through negotiation and custom rather than written deeds. This distinction would later prove disastrous.

In the Chesapeake region, the Powhatan Confederacy was among the most politically centralized Indigenous systems encountered by Europeans. Dozens of communities were bound together by tribute, alliance, and force, forming a regional power that initially dictated the terms of English survival in Virginia. Along the Eastern Shore and upriver, other nations navigated the expanding gravitational pull of English settlement.

This diversity matters. There was no single "Native response" to colonization because there was no single Native world to begin with.

Contact Was Not a Moment

The term "contact" suggests a single encounter: ships arriving, hands shaking, worlds meeting. In reality, contact was a process that unfolded unevenly over decades—and often began before sustained settlement took root.

Early Atlantic Contacts

Seasonal European fishing fleets began working the rich cod grounds off Newfoundland and the Grand Banks in the late 1400s, with English, French, Spanish, and Portuguese crews crossing the Atlantic every summer.[1] In the late 1400s and early 1500s, Iberian and later English and French expeditions began crossing the Atlantic, initially seeking routes to Asia and valuable resources.

These fishermen came ashore to dry fish, cut timber, and take on water. In some places, this meant trading in fish, furs, and tools; in others, Indigenous peoples such as the

Beothuk tried to avoid face-to-face meetings and instead scavenged abandoned European fishing stations.[2]

By the late 1500s, hundreds of boats sailed into these waters each year. European presence shifted from short, sporadic visits to more organized ventures centered on trade. Fur traders in the north established posts and relied on Indigenous partners who supplied pelts, food, geographic knowledge, and military support, while receiving metal tools, cloth, and other goods that were integrated into Native economies and diplomacy.

Missionaries, especially Spanish in the south and French in the north, established missions that were often the first permanent European institutions in some regions, introducing new religious pressures and attempting to gather Indigenous people into mission towns. These missions, posts, and small forts became places where languages, beliefs, and technologies mixed, and where alliances and rivalries between Indigenous nations and European powers first sparked conflict and compromise.

Colonies and Contagions

Permanent colonies quickly followed: Jamestown in 1607, Quebec in 1608, and Plymouth in 1620, with further English settlements in New England and along the mid-Atlantic coast through the 1600s. New Netherland was founded by the Dutch in 1624, with New Amsterdam established in 1625; the English colony of Maryland was established in 1632–1634, each tightening European claims on Indigenous homelands.

These colonies arrived not as neutral neighbors but as expansionist systems fueled by land hunger. They claimed land, demanded labor or tribute, and drew Indigenous nations into European wars and imperial rivalries, even as Native communities tried to keep their distance. European concepts of property, sovereignty, and inheritance were fundamentally incompatible with Indigenous land use and governance. Oral and conditional agreements were later recorded as permanent transfers. Alliances forged for survival were treated as submissions.

Trade further complicated the landscape. Metal tools, firearms, and cloth reshaped daily life and warfare, creating dependencies that European powers exploited. Control of trade networks became as critical as control of territory. Indigenous leaders were forced to balance immediate material needs with long-term autonomy, often without knowing which choice would be fatal.

Pathogens traveled along the same networks: Native traders who met Europeans on the seacoast or in early mission settlements could carry measles, influenza, and smallpox to distant villages days or weeks away, long before anyone in those communities ever saw a European face.

Smallpox became one of the most destabilizing forces in the Atlantic homelands, as epidemic disease preceded large-scale settlement, weakening communities before they fully understood the source of the catastrophe. The demographic losses reshaped politics: succession crises emerged, towns consolidated or relocated, alliances shifted, and the balance of power among neighboring nations changed.

These epidemics also intensified colonial pressure. As populations fell and communities were forced to reorganize, Europeans increasingly treated disrupted land use as abandonment. They used disease-driven instability to push for land cessions, "protections," or permanent settlement.

The first major smallpox pandemic in the Americas swept out from the Caribbean around 1518–1525, killing enormous numbers of Indigenous people on the islands and then in Mesoamerica, where one epidemic in 1520–1521 may have killed a third to half of the population. Through the 1500s and early 1600s, waves of smallpox, measles, influenza, and other infections continued to strike Native communities across the hemisphere, often in rapid succession, leaving no time for recovery between outbreaks.

In eastern North America, for example, a devastating epidemic—sometimes called "the Great Dying"—swept through Indigenous villages in southern New England between 1616 and 1619, likely killing the majority of people in some coastal areas several years before the Mayflower arrived in 1620.[3]

By the mid-1600s, repeated epidemics had already reshaped the human landscape in many regions, leaving behind what later colonists wrongly imagined to be "empty" or "widowed" lands.

Political and Social Fallout

These losses did more than reduce numbers; they undermined governance and social stability across many

Indigenous nations. Deaths among elders, healers, warriors, and diplomatic leaders disrupted the transmission of knowledge, weakened existing alliances, and opened the door to internal tensions and external pressures.

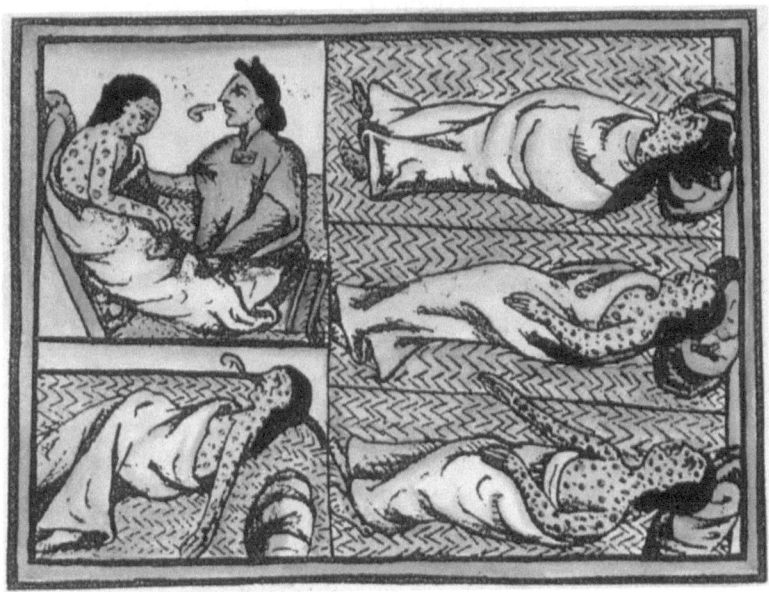

Smallpox! Original illustration by unknown 16th-century artist, Public Domain.

With fewer people to hunt, farm, or trade, and with neighboring groups suffering unevenly, competition for remaining hunting grounds, trade routes, and safe territories often intensified. Treaties were negotiated by communities still reeling from population loss. Wars were fought by nations already weakened by illness. Alliances were forged in a landscape where survival itself had become uncertain.

By the time sustained colonization accelerated along the Atlantic coast, Indigenous societies had already endured a demographic and political shock that fundamentally altered the terms of contact.

Leadership Under Pressure

Indigenous leadership was tested not only by external threats but also by internal strain. Population loss had weakened traditional authority, and younger leaders challenged elders. Factions emerged over whether to resist, negotiate, relocate, or align with one colonial power against another. These divisions were not signs of weakness; they were symptoms of societies under unprecedented stress.

Colonial records often portray Native leaders as inconsistent or unreliable for failing to deliver permanent outcomes. This misrepresents Indigenous political reality. Chiefs were accountable to councils and communities, not empowered to bind their people indefinitely. A treaty made under duress did not erase future resistance. Accommodation did not signal surrender.

Leaders were forced to operate within these constraints. They were not free agents. They were mediators between worlds, responsible for immediate survival and long-term continuity in circumstances that allowed for neither certainty nor safety.

A Shared Turning Point

What united the Atlantic Homelands was not culture, language, or political structure but timing. These nations faced the earliest and most sustained pressures of European colonization. The decisions made along the coast— alliances formed, wars fought, treaties signed, migrations forced—shaped the trajectory of colonization across the continent.

As European expansion reached inland in force, the Atlantic world had already been transformed. The strategies that succeeded or failed there became precedents elsewhere. The cost of miscalculation was already evident.

Across the continent, Indigenous peoples blended older traditions with new realities—reshaping economies, diplomacy, and spiritual life—so that, even after centuries of upheaval, their communities, languages, and political goals endure today. This broader story of contact is one of profound loss but also of ongoing negotiation, survival, and creativity in the face of rapidly changing forces.

Their stories, and the stories of the leaders who follow, are rooted in the world outlined here—a world that did not vanish with contact, but was irrevocably altered by it.

[1] Cornelius J. Jaenen, Friend and Foe: Aspects of French–Amerindian Cultural Contact in the Sixteenth and Seventeenth Centuries (Toronto: McClelland and Stewart, 1976), 98–99.
[2] Colin G. Calloway, First Peoples: A Documentary Survey of American Indian History (Baltimore: Johns Hopkins University Press, 1997).
[3] Heather Whipps, "How Smallpox Changed the World," LiveScience, June 23, 2008.

Membertou

Sakmow, Mi'kmaq First Nations

1507 – 18 September 1611

Chapter 2 — Membertou, Mi'kmaq Nation

Do not speak of owning the land, for the land owns your breath, your dreams, your silence.

— Indigenous Teaching

Membertou and the Atlantic World

WHEN EUROPEANS ENCOUNTERED THE Mi'kmaq Nation in the early sixteenth century, they did not meet a people unfamiliar with outsiders. For generations before permanent settlement, Mi'kmaq communities had navigated an Atlantic world already in motion—seasonal fishing fleets, traders, and missionaries arriving and departing along the coast. By the time sustained contact began, diplomacy was not new. What was new was scale, permanence, and consequence.

Membertou emerged as a leader in this shifting world. As a sagamaw (District Chief) of the Mi'kmaq, his authority rested not on coercion but on reputation, kinship ties, spiritual standing, and the ability to act decisively in moments of crisis. He presided over a region where leadership was earned through persuasion, wisdom, and a lifetime of tested judgment. Among the Mi'kmaq, this authority was a delicate balance between the independence of local clans and the cohesion of a broader alliance. A leader succeeded not by decree but by sustaining consensus, a task that demanded both strength and subtlety.

Membertou's leadership coincided with one of the region's most volatile periods: epidemic disease, intensifying European rivalry, and the first sustained efforts to convert alliance into control.

A Maritime Nation

The Mi'kmaq occupied a vast coastal and riverine territory spanning what is now Nova Scotia, Prince Edward Island, and parts of New Brunswick and the Gaspé Peninsula. Their society was built around the sea. Seasonal movement among fishing grounds, inland hunting territories, and winter settlements structured daily life and political relationships. Mobility was not disorder; it was strategy.

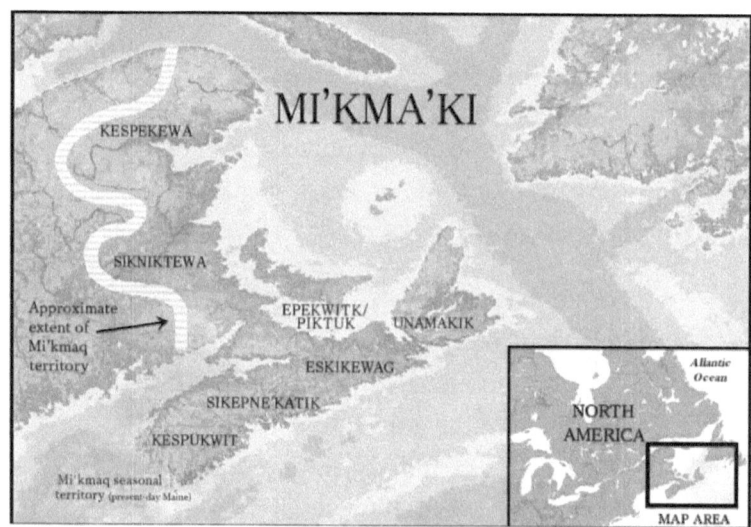

Mi'kmaq Territory

By the early 1600s, epidemics had already altered the demographic landscape of the Northeast. Although precise numbers are difficult to establish, population loss was significant enough to destabilize communities and strain leadership structures. Membertou's authority was exercised in a world already narrowed by loss, where survival required adaptation rather than isolation.

The French Arrive

In the summer of 1534, Jacques Cartier sailed into the cold, fog-laced waters of the Gulf of St. Lawrence with a narrow mandate and wide ambitions. France sought a western passage to Asia, a foothold in the Atlantic fishery, and intelligence on land, people, and profit. Cartier found no shortcut to Cathay, but he did find something just as valuable: Indigenous nations already fluent in the rhythms of Atlantic exchange.

Along the coasts and river mouths, Cartier's crews encountered people accustomed to European ships and goods, wary but not alarmed. Trade was tentative and ceremonial rather than hostile—iron for furs, gestures for meaning. Cartier claimed land for the French crown with a raised cross, but the act carried little immediate weight. What mattered more was the quiet realization on both sides that the Atlantic world had arrived and was not leaving.

Over the next seventy years, that contact hardened into routine. European fishermen returned season after season, and traders followed. By the time the French crown sanctioned a permanent settlement in Acadia, the encounter was no longer novel—it was strategic.

In 1604, Pierre Dugua de Mons and Samuel de Champlain arrived to plant France's flag in the borderlands of what is now Maine and Nova Scotia. Their first attempt on the St. Croix River nearly killed them. The winter was brutal, supplies failed, and scurvy did what no enemy could. Survival required local knowledge, alliances, and humility—qualities colonial ventures rarely brought but quickly learned to adopt.

That lesson came into full focus in 1605, when the French began rebuilding at Port-Royal and encountered Membertou. This was not a "first contact" meeting but a reckoning between seasoned coastal peoples and desperate newcomers. Membertou understood the newcomers immediately: their power, their fragility, and their usefulness. The French wanted stability, food, and furs; they needed allies more than land.

Membertou

Born around 1507, Membertou rose to prominence in a coastal world already shaped by contact. He was sakmow—grand chief—of the Mi'kmaq, based near Port Royal in what is now Nova Scotia. His authority began in the Kespukwitk district, but it soon extended beyond it. The sakmowk of the Mi'kmaq's other six districts elevated him to grand chief, recognizing a leader capable of navigating a changing Atlantic world.

Membertou understood the sea as both a boundary and an opportunity. Unlike many Indigenous leaders whose contact with Europeans remained coastal and controlled, he pushed outward. He acquired his own French shallop, a small, fast, and unmistakably foreign vessel, which he marked with personal totems and used as an extension of his authority. With it, he sailed beyond the shoreline to meet European traders before they reached land.

The advantage was decisive. By trading at sea, Membertou controlled access to markets and information, positioning himself ahead of rivals and middlemen alike. Goods passed through his hands first, on terms he dictated. In a world where power increasingly followed commerce, Membertou did not wait for Europeans to come ashore. He met them on the water—and for a time, he set the terms.

In the summer of 1534, when Jacques Cartier entered the Gulf of St. Lawrence, it was Membertou who greeted him. The encounter was formal and transactional. Cartier came seeking passage, wealth, and claim; Membertou assessed this new kind of visitor with caution. Gifts were exchanged, intentions weighed, and each side departed believing it had gained understanding. Cartier would remember the meeting as discovery. Membertou understood it as reconnaissance, the first measure of a foreign power that would return in greater numbers and with greater demands.

Membertou offered hospitality and an alliance on Mi'kmaq terms, allowing Habitation at Port-Royal by incorporating it into an Indigenous world that had already learned to absorb outsiders without surrendering control. The future of Acadia would be written in that balance—between accommodation and resistance, and between diplomacy and survival—and Membertou stood at its center.

Maintaining that balance proved difficult. Trade could strengthen a community, but it could also undermine self-sufficiency. Alliances could deter aggression, but they could also invite retaliation. There was no neutral position once European powers committed to permanent settlement.

When the French withdrew in 1607, it was not defeat by arms that drove them out but the collapse of their royal trading monopoly. Port-Royal, barely established, was abandoned almost as abruptly as it had been built. Two Frenchmen were left behind to watch the Habitation—an extraordinary vote of trust in a land Europeans still liked to describe as wild. During those three years of absence, Membertou ensured the place endured.

The Habitation of Port Royal

Membertou, who was more than 100 years old by all accounts, guarded the fort, protected the men, and treated the abandoned French structures not as spoils but as obligations. When the French ships finally returned in 1610, Membertou was there to meet them, with the Habitation intact. In a world where European colonies routinely vanished without a trace, this continuity mattered.

It told the French exactly who their most reliable partner was.

What followed was less a religious awakening than a calculated public act. On Saint John the Baptist Day, June 24, 1610, Membertou presented himself for baptism. A priest performed the ceremony, baptizing Membertou and twenty-one members of his immediate family. Membertou took the name Henri in honor of the recently assassinated King Henry IV of France. To French observers, this was a triumph: the conversion of a powerful Indigenous leader, proof that empire and salvation could advance together.

But to read it only that way is to miss the point. Baptism functioned as diplomacy. It formalized an alliance, affirmed mutual obligation, and placed the French squarely within a Mi'kmaq framework of relationship rather than conquest.

This moment became the foundation of what later scholars would call the Mi'kmaw Concordat—a durable, negotiated relationship with the Catholic Church that emphasized alliance rather than submission. Membertou did not abandon his authority or worldview; he incorporated new rituals into an existing leadership system that had always adapted to changing circumstances.

There is no evidence that conversion erased Mi'kmaq spiritual practices or political autonomy. Indigenous leaders across the Atlantic world selectively adopted elements of European religion when it served strategic ends, often integrating them into existing belief systems rather than replacing them. Membertou's decision should be read as pragmatic leadership under constraint, not as cultural abandonment.

For the French at Port-Royal, the message was clear. Their survival depended not on forts or flags but on the consent and cooperation of the people who already knew the land. In the early Atlantic world, power belonged not only to those who arrived by ship but also to those who knew how to make newcomers stay—on Indigenous terms.

Throughout this period, Mi'kmaq resistance did not disappear. It shifted form. Raiding, negotiation, withdrawal, and selective engagement were all tools employed to preserve autonomy. Colonial sources often record these actions as inconsistent. In reality, they were adaptive responses to rapidly changing threats.

Leadership at the Edge of Permanence

Membertou did not live to see the full consequences of European colonization in the region.

In the late summer of 1611, the Atlantic bargain revealed its cost. Membertou fell ill with dysentery, one of the invisible weapons Europeans carried with them wherever they went—diseases that traveled faster and killed more efficiently than muskets. By September, he was gravely weakened. The sickness that took him was not Mi'kmaq in origin; it belonged to the new world being stitched together by ships, trade, and proximity: dysentery.

As his strength failed, Membertou initially asked to be buried with his ancestors, as was the custom of his people. The missionaries were troubled. They had come to see his conversion as a cornerstone of French hopes in Acadia, and a traditional burial threatened to undermine its meaning.

Then, in a final turn that reflected the same political clarity that had guided his life, Membertou changed his request. He asked instead to be buried among the French. It was not a repudiation of his past but a deliberate closing gesture— one last affirmation of alliance.

On September 18, 1611, he died, urging his children with his final words to remain devout Christians. The French mourned him as a protector and patron; the Mi'kmaq mourned him as a leader who had navigated the most dangerous transition their world had yet faced. Membertou did not live to see what that transition would bring, but he understood its stakes. In choosing where he would lie in death, he left behind a message as clear as any treaty: coexistence had been possible—briefly, precariously—and it had depended, above all, on his judgment.

French Acadia

Membertou's alliance gave the French something no charter in Paris could guarantee: time. In the first decades of Acadia, when Port-Royal was less a colony than a fragile outpost, French survival hinged on Indigenous diplomacy—access to food in lean seasons, safe movement through contested waterways, and a political place in a region where power already had owners.

Membertou's decision to treat the Habitation as a partner rather than a target established a pattern other Mi'kmaq leaders could extend: alliance as a relationship of reciprocity, not submission. It also gave French officials and missionaries a working model for how influence actually spread in North America: not through proclamations, but through trust earned, renewed, and enforced by leaders who could say yes—or withdraw consent.

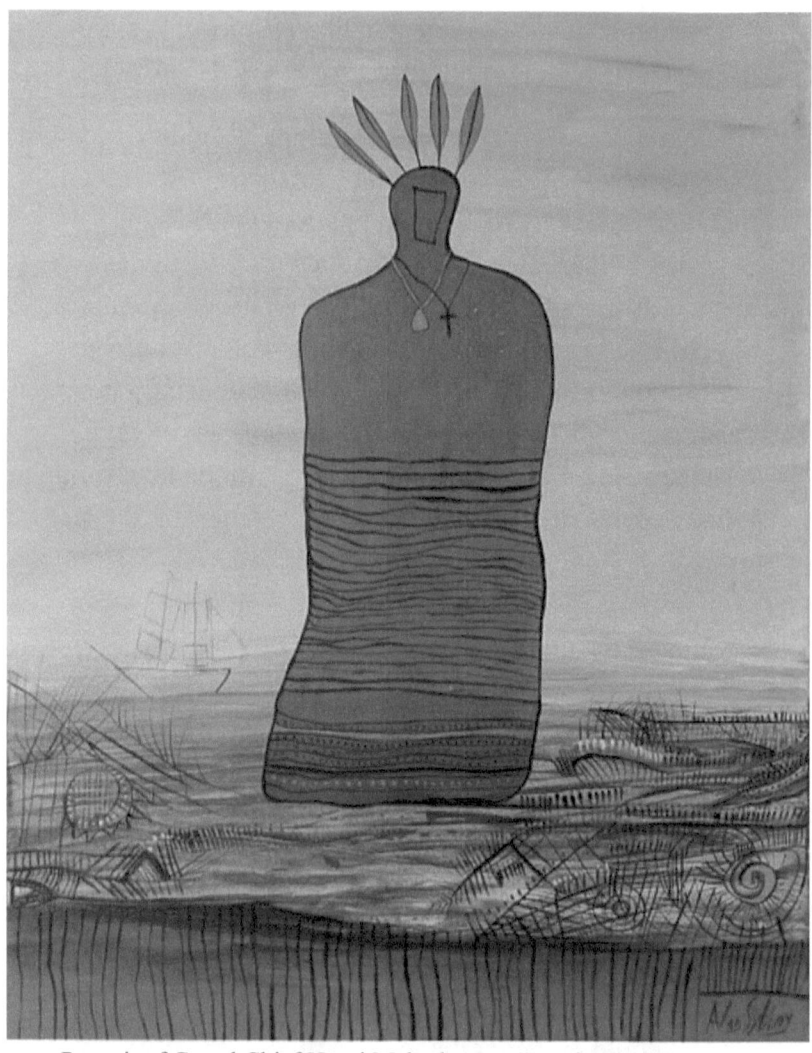

Portrait of Grand Chief Henri Mebmbertou, By Alan Sylliboy

Over the generations that followed, French–Mi'kmaq alliances reshaped the northeastern frontier into something closer to a negotiated borderland than a clean line on a map. With Mi'kmaq support, the French could contest English expansion far beyond what their small numbers should have allowed, while the Mi'kmaq leveraged French trade goods, military partnership, and diplomatic recognition to defend their own autonomy against growing pressure.

The result was a different balance of power along the coast and river corridors of the northeast—one where English settlements could not assume easy dominance and where French presence, though often thin, remained stubbornly durable.

The alliance did not freeze history in place; it bought leverage. And in a region where empires rose and fell on the strength of relationships with Native nations, Membertou's early choices echoed long after his death—in the wars that followed, the trade networks that endured, and the simple fact that the French were still there to matter.

Before Borders

The northeastern frontier did not develop as an open field for English settlement; it emerged as a contested, negotiated space where Indigenous power mattered. Mi'kmaq diplomacy helped anchor the French presence in the region and prevented any single European power from moving unchecked along the coast and through the interior waterways. This slowed English expansion northward and eastward, forcing New England colonies to grow inward and southward instead. The map that would eventually define the northeastern United States owes as much to Indigenous resistance and alliance-building as to European ambition.

The French–Mi'kmaq alliance ensured that the northeast remained a pressure point rather than a prize easily claimed, influencing decades of colonial conflict and negotiation. In that sense, Mi'kmaq history is not a sidebar to American history; it is part of its foundation. The United States emerged not from empty land, but from landscapes already defended, negotiated, and shaped by nations like the Mi'kmaq, whose decisions altered the course of empire long before there was an America to inherit it.

Legacy

Membertou is remembered as a transitional figure, standing at the threshold between two worlds. The choices Membertou made were not endpoints but attempts to shape outcomes in a world where the terms of engagement were constantly shifting. Later generations would reassess those choices as their conditions worsened and accommodation yielded diminishing returns.

What Membertou represents is not acquiescence but the limits of early diplomacy. His leadership illustrates a moment when engagement still held the promise of coexistence, before settlement hardened into dispossession and alliance into control. That moment was brief.

Understanding Membertou requires rejecting the simplicity of triumph or tragedy. He was neither a collaborator nor a romantic hero. He was a leader under unprecedented pressure, using the tools at hand to secure his people's future in an uncertain Atlantic world.

He was able to navigate competing worlds without losing sight of his own. His prominence was not a gift of birthright but of proven leadership—an earned trust from those who depended on his experience to interpret the shifting winds of history. In him, the Mi'kmaq found a leader capable of bridging tradition and change with a steadiness that would shape the course of his people's future.

2007 Canadian stamp, "French Settlement in North America" series, in honor of Chief Membertou.

Madockawando

Sachem, Penobscot

1630 -1698

Chapter 3—Madockawando, Penobscot Nation

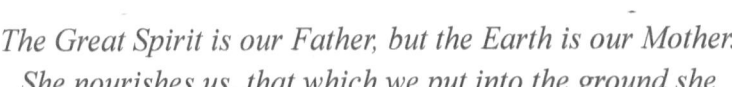

The Great Spirit is our Father, but the Earth is our Mother. She nourishes us, that which we put into the ground she returns to us.

— Big Thunder (Frank Loring), Penobscot

The Limits of Alliance

BY THE TIME MADOCKAWANDO emerged as a Penobscot sachem, the Atlantic world Membertou had navigated was already changing. What had once been a fluid zone of seasonal trade and tentative diplomacy was hardening into something more dangerous: permanent settlement, a growing military presence, and open competition for land. The possibilities of coexistence were narrowing, and the costs of miscalculation were rising. Madockawando's leadership unfolded in this altered landscape.

Born in 1630 in what is now Maine, Madockawando faced a reality in which alliances failed as often as they protected. His career marks the transition from conditional engagement to sustained resistance in the northeastern borderlands.

The Failure of Accommodation

By the time of Madockawando's prominence, the limits of earlier accommodation were evident. Alliances forged for mutual benefit were reinterpreted by colonial authorities as submission. Treaties were enforced selectively or ignored altogether. Indigenous compliance was expected without reciprocal restraint.

This shift transformed leadership. Diplomacy remained necessary, but it could no longer be the primary strategy. Leaders had to balance negotiation with force and flexibility with resolve. Those who failed to adapt risked being rendered irrelevant—or erased.

The Penobscot Homeland

The Penobscot people occupied a strategic and contested region centered on the Penobscot River and its tributaries in what is now central Maine. The river was more than a geographic feature. It was a transportation artery, a food source, and a political boundary connecting inland forests to the Atlantic coast. Control of this corridor meant access to trade and influence over movement through the region.

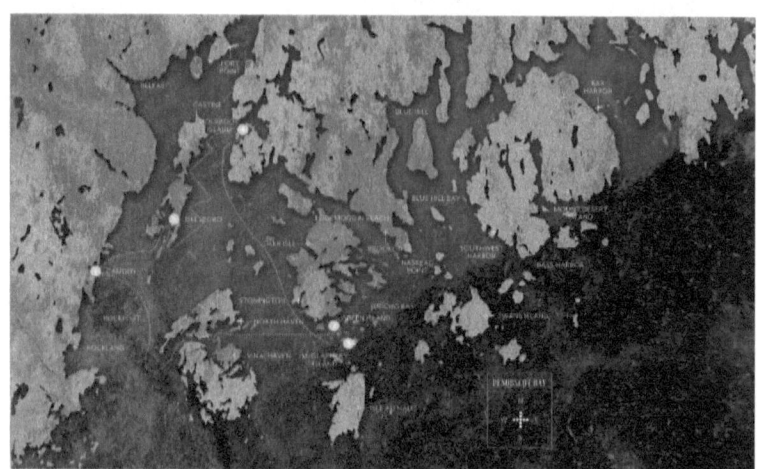

Like other Wabanaki nations, the Penobscot organized life around seasonal cycles and mobility. Villages moved with the seasons, and leadership relied on persuasion, kinship, and proven judgment. Authority was earned, not imposed. Madockawando's prominence suggests a leader whose decisions resonated in a time when survival demanded clarity of purpose.

A Borderland Under Pressure

Maine in the late seventeenth century was a borderland shaped by imperial rivalry. Claimed by both France and England, it in truth belonged to neither—it was Penobscot country, threaded with deep forests, tidal inlets, and villages bound by kinship.

French and English interests overlapped and clashed, drawing Indigenous nations into conflicts that were neither brief nor localized. Alliances shifted as circumstances changed, but the underlying pressure remained constant: European expansion demanded land, and once settlement took root, withdrawal was rare.

Unlike the earlier period of contact, when trade relationships were managed without permanent occupation, English settlement increasingly brought fences, forts, and claims of ownership. The assumption that land could be enclosed and permanently transferred through written agreements clashed directly with Indigenous land use and governance. Negotiations no longer occurred on equal terms.

Modackawando

Born in Maine around 1630, Madockawando stood at the fault line of an Atlantic war he had not chosen. As chief of the Penobscot, his authority spanned Maine territory that had become contested ground between English New England and French Acadia. For decades, Madockawando navigated this pressure by deliberately aligning with the French, whose trading posts and Jesuit missions offered an alliance without immediate dispossession. Raids, reprisals, and shifting borders followed, drawing the Penobscot deeper into imperial conflict. When the war ended with the Treaty of Breda, it reshaped power in the Northeast without Native consent, ceding Acadia to France while leaving English settlers entrenched. Madockawando was forced to reckon with a new reality: Indigenous survival would now depend on negotiating outcomes decided an ocean away.

War

When King Philip's War erupted across southern New England, the conflict drew in the eastern Wabanaki world, pulling the Penobscot and the scattered English settlements of Maine and New Hampshire into a war they had neither started nor could avoid. What had begun as a localized uprising against English encroachment became, by late 1675, a regional struggle for survival, sovereignty, and control of the frontier. English settlers along the Maine coast suddenly found themselves exposed—thinly spread, poorly defended, and dependent on alliances that were never as secure as they believed.

Seeking to limit destruction and preserve their people, the Penobscot were the first Native nation in the region to sue for peace. In November 1676, Madockawando traveled to Boston to formalize an agreement with English authorities. Articles of peace were drafted and signed, and the settlement was ratified in the name of stability and coexistence. On paper, it looked like reconciliation. In practice, it proved fragile. The English soon manufactured a pretext to reopen hostilities—an all-too-familiar pattern in frontier diplomacy, where treaties held only as long as they constrained Native power without inconveniencing colonial ambition.

Resistance as Strategy

The response was decisive. The Penobscot did not collapse under renewed pressure; they countered. English settlements across that portion of Maine were overrun and destroyed, erasing years of colonial advance in a single, violent reversal. What followed was not chaos but consequence: all English settlements were destroyed.

The destruction underscored a truth English authorities repeatedly underestimated: peace without respect was temporary, and Native nations retained the capacity to defend their homelands when pushed beyond endurance. Along the northeastern frontier, settlement did not advance in a straight line. It lurched, stalled, and sometimes vanished entirely—shaped as much by Wabanaki resistance as by English persistence.

The war-weary frontier settled, briefly, into an uneasy calm in 1678 with the Treaty of Casco, an agreement that revealed the true balance of power in coastal Maine. English settlers were permitted to return to their abandoned farms—but only on Penobscot terms. Rent was to be paid to the Penobscot, a blunt acknowledgment that English occupation rested on Indigenous consent, not entitlement.

For a decade, the peace largely held. Farms were rebuilt, trade resumed, and the frontier functioned not as an English possession but as a negotiated landscape where Native authority remained visible and enforceable.

That balance was shattered in 1688, when imperial rivalry replaced restraint. Edmund Andros, the Crown's agent, arrived among the Penobscot in an unmistakable display of force. He sacked the house of Madockawando's daughter. The act was more than vandalism; it was a declaration. Andros signaled that English authority would no longer tolerate French influence or Indigenous independence along the frontier. The Penobscot chiefs understood immediately what was at stake.

The response was swift and organized. Supplied with arms by allies, the chiefs took up the fight and turned again on English settlements. Villages were attacked, farms destroyed (again), and the frontier was thrown back into war. These clashes became one of the regional sparks for King William's War, part of a much larger English-French struggle for empire. While European crowns framed the war as a contest between nations, on the ground, it was a fight over influence, alliance, and survival.

Madockawando emerged once again as a central figure, playing a prominent role at every major stage of the conflict. For the Penobscot, war was not an interruption of history—it was the cost of refusing to be absorbed by it.

By 1693, exhaustion and calculation pushed the English once more toward diplomacy. They secured Madockawando's consent to a new treaty of peace, hoping that his authority could quiet the northeastern frontier as it had before. But the political landscape had shifted.

By now, Madockawando no longer spoke for a unified coalition. Other chiefs, bound by alliance and faith to French Jesuit emissaries of the Society of Jesus, rejected the agreement outright. The divide was not simply religious; it reflected competing strategies for survival in a tightening imperial vise. Unable to impose unity where it no longer existed, Madockawando was compelled to resume hostilities—less by choice than by the reality that peace without consensus was impossible.

Even when Europe moved on, the frontier did not. Fighting in the northeast dragged on more than a year after France and England formally ended their war with the Peace of Ryswick.

For Indigenous nations, European treaties often arrived late, if at all, and rarely reflected conditions on the ground. Sometime during this final phase, Madockawando withdrew from the Maine coast to Meductic, a Maliseet-Abenaki mission village along the St. John River. Like Membertou before him, Madockawando did not fall in battle. In 1698, he died in a smallpox epidemic—another reminder that disease, not diplomacy, was often the most decisive force of the age.

Legacy

Colonial records often frame Madockawando as a hostile figure, emphasizing raids and conflict. This framing reflects European priorities rather than Indigenous strategy. For the Penobscot and their allies, resistance was not impulsive violence but a calculated response to encroachment that diplomacy had failed to halt.

Madockawando

Raiding temporarily disrupted settlement, challenged assumptions of security, and signaled that land claims were contested. It also served as a means of defending territory in the absence of formal armies or fortified towns. In a world where European powers were unwilling to recognize Indigenous sovereignty, resistance became one of the few remaining tools available.

Madockawando's actions were not isolated. They occurred within a broader Wabanaki resistance that included the Mi'kmaq, Passamaquoddy, and Abenaki, and they were often coordinated with French interests—not out of loyalty, but out of necessity. Alliance with the French offered weapons, trade goods, and a counterweight to English expansion. It did not guarantee protection.

Madockawando understood that resistance could delay dispossession, but it could not reverse the demographic and military imbalance in favor of the European powers. Still, delay mattered. Each season gained preserved land, autonomy, and the possibility—however fragile—of a different outcome. His resistance slowed expansion, shaped colonial strategy, and preserved Penobscot identity amid sustained pressure.

Madockawando's story is not one of inevitability. It is a record of resistance and of leadership that refused to accept disappearance as a foregone conclusion.

The Penobscot did not disappear. They endured through adaptation, relocation, and continued assertion of sovereignty. Madockawando's leadership belongs to that longer story—not as a final stand, but as part of an ongoing struggle that extended beyond his lifetime.

From Diplomacy to Defense

Taken together, the lives of Membertou and Madockawando illustrate the narrowing choices faced by Indigenous leaders in the Atlantic homelands. Where early contact allowed for cautious optimism, later decades demanded harder decisions. Diplomacy did not vanish, but it no longer stood alone.

The chapters that follow move south and inland, tracing how similar pressures played out among different nations and leaders. The patterns will repeat, but the responses will vary—shaped by geography, timing, and the character of leadership under strain.

Part II— Southern New England: Wampanoag and
Narragansett

Chapter 4 — Power, Pressure, and the Illusion of Settlement

*They have a partial, if not a covetous eye upon our land,
and their desire is to have it all. They say it is their God
who has given it to them, but we know it is our own.*

—Miantonomi, Narragansett Sachem

SOUTHERN NEW ENGLAND WAS one of the most
densely populated and politically complex Indigenous
regions on the Atlantic coast at the time of European
contact. The area encompassing present-day Massachusetts,
Rhode Island, and Connecticut supported interlinked
Native nations whose economies, diplomacy, and rivalries
were finely balanced. Control of land and waterways was
carefully negotiated, and leadership was exercised through
consensus, kinship, and long-standing custom.

When English colonists arrived in the early seventeenth
century, they did not encounter an unclaimed landscape.
They entered a region already structured by Indigenous
law.

A Crowded and Connected World

Southern New England's geography encouraged
concentration. Fertile soil, abundant fisheries, and
navigable rivers supported large populations and sustained

agriculture. Coastal and inland communities were connected by trade routes that extended deep into the interior, linking this region to the Hudson Valley, the Connecticut River basin, and beyond.

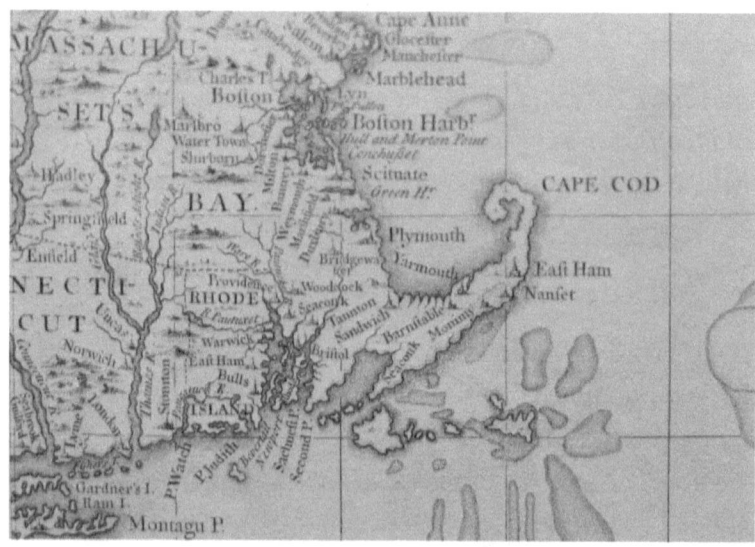
Southern New England

Along the outer elbow of Cape Cod and down through the islands and bays, the Wampanoag world was a chain of closely related communities—Nauset on the Cape, Patuxet around the deep-water coves of what became Plymouth, and the Pokanoket centered farther southwest around Mount Hope and Narragansett Bay. They shared language and kinship with their neighbors, and they shared something else: a coastline that made them early witnesses to the Atlantic's new traffic—fishing crews, traders, shipwrecked strangers, and, eventually, permanent settlers.

The shore fed them and exposed them. It offered wealth in fish and shellfish and wampum-making materials, but it also opened the door to epidemics and to the relentless pressure of English towns that arrived with fences, courts, and paper claims.

To the west, the Narragansett held the best natural fortress in southern New England: the bays, coves, and islands that could hide canoes, concentrate trade, and control the flow of people and news. Their power rested less on a single "capital" than on a dense web of villages, tribute relationships, and alliances that could be expanded or tightened as circumstances demanded. Nearby, the Niantic—often described as having Eastern and Western branches—occupied the seam between shore and interior, a people positioned to mediate coastal exchange and inland politics. In this corridor, diplomacy was never abstract. It was a day-to-day calculation of who could be trusted, whose marriages mattered, which trails were safe, and how a new English fort or trading house would affect the balance.

Farther south and west, along the rivers and in the thick woods of what became Connecticut, the map shows a set of overlapping homelands: Pequot, Mohegan, Quinnipiac, Paugussett, Potatuck, Podunk, Tunxis (with the Massaco often named alongside them), and the river peoples sometimes grouped under labels like Wangunk and Mattabeset. These were not isolated "tribes" sitting still on a textbook map. They were communities tied to specific river systems—the Thames, Quinnipiac, Housatonic, and

Connecticut—whose leaders managed access to planting grounds, fishing places, and trade routes.

The rivers were both highways and boundaries. Control of them meant influence; losing them meant hunger, dispersal, and dependence. As English settlement expanded, older rivalries could be sharpened into weapons, and older alliances could become lifelines—because proximity to the newcomers could bring leverage one year and disaster the next.

Inland, the corridor between the coast and the Hudson was home to the Nipmuc in the interior uplands; the Massachusett and their communities, such as the Ponkapoag, around the Boston basin; the Pennacook along the Merrimack watershed; the Pocumtuc in the Connecticut River valley around rich planting land; and, farther west, peoples of the upper Hudson edge, such as the Schaghticoke and the Mahican, later associated with Stockbridge and, in the long aftermath of displacement, with the Stockbridge–Munsee community.

This is the bridge into New York: a world where river valleys connected empires—English coastal towns, Dutch and later English Hudson settlements, and French influence from the north—and where Native communities were forced into the role of geographical strategists. The same trails that once carried trade and visiting parties began carrying refugees. The same rivers that once measured seasonal abundance began measuring the pace of colonial expansion.

Political authority was decentralized rather than centralized, with sachems relying on councils and alliances to maintain stability. Competition was constant yet regulated. Warfare occurred, but it followed established norms. Balance mattered. No single nation dominated the region for long without provoking resistance. This balance would not survive colonization.

Massachusetts, 1620

By the time English settlers established Plymouth in 1620, Southern New England had already suffered catastrophic population loss from epidemic disease. Outbreaks in the years immediately preceding settlement—most notably between roughly 1616 and 1619—devastated coastal and nearby inland communities.

Estimates vary, but published mortality figures range from about one-third to as high as 90 percent in the affected region.[1] The result was widespread depopulation and consolidation: entire villages were abandoned or forced to merge with neighboring communities. Political authority was disrupted precisely as foreign settlements began to take root.

These losses reshaped the political landscape. Succession lines were broken, power shifted among nations, and long-standing rivalries intensified as communities struggled to recover. English settlers misread the signs of collapse— empty places, disrupted fields, fewer people—as abandonment or providence rather than the aftermath of biological catastrophe. The timing mattered. Colonization began not at the height of Indigenous strength but in the wake of profound destabilization.

English Settlement as a New Force

Unlike earlier European visitors, English settlers arrived with the intent to stay. They brought families, livestock, fences, and an assumption of permanent land ownership. Their concept of settlement was incompatible with Indigenous land use, which emphasized shared access, seasonal movement, and negotiated boundaries.

Early English survival, however, depended almost entirely on Indigenous knowledge and restraint. The settlers who arrived along the New England coast brought tools, weapons, and written claims, but little understanding of the land they intended to occupy. They arrived too late in the season to plant. They did not know which crops would thrive in coastal soil, how long the winters could last, or where reliable fresh water could be found once surface streams froze. Many were already weakened by disease and months at sea.

The great irony is that without Indigenous assistance, the colonies would not have lasted a year. The English survived their first winters because Native communities intervened—sometimes deliberately, sometimes reluctantly. Food was shared when starvation loomed. Corn was traded not merely as a commodity but as knowledge: how to plant, store, and prepare it so it sustained rather than sickened. Indigenous guides showed settlers where to fish, where shellfish could be found even in winter, and how to navigate forests that, to the English, seemed trackless and hostile.

Diplomacy mattered as much as sustenance. Indigenous leaders chose not to exploit English weakness in the earliest years, even when they could have done so. Settlements were vulnerable, poorly defended, and internally divided. Violence at that moment would have been decisive. Instead, coexistence—however cautious—was allowed to take root.

Trade agreements formalized these relationships. European metal goods, cloth, and tools entered Indigenous economies, while food and local knowledge flowed in the opposite direction. These exchanges were not acts of charity. They were political decisions, shaped by existing rivalries and strategic calculations. Indigenous leaders assessed the newcomers not as masters but as another power to be managed.

Yet from the beginning, the two sides were operating under incompatible assumptions.

A Long History of Conquest

Europeans did not arrive on the Atlantic coast as blank-slate farmers. They arrived with a political inheritance shaped by centuries of conquest, dispossession, and legal absorption of defeated peoples. In their world, land changed hands through force and was then stabilized through paperwork—charters, titles, and courts. The Normans had conquered England in 1066 and redistributed land through feudal tenure. Long before that, Rome had conquered much of Britain, crushing resistance—famously including the rebellion associated with the Iceni—and folding territory into an imperial system of taxation, roads, and law. Across the medieval and early modern periods,

European states refined a repeating pattern: claim, subdue, settle, and legalize.

That habit of expansion matured into an ideology. By the time English settlers crossed the Atlantic, "improvement" was treated as proof of rightful possession: land fenced, planted, and "made productive" was considered owned in a way that seasonal use and shared access were not.

European monarchs issued charters that treated distant territory as property to be granted before any negotiation with the people living there. Conquest did not require extermination to be considered complete; it required replacing one system of law with another. Once a claim was written, it could be defended in court, enforced by militia, and extended by the steady arrival of settlers.

In that sense, the Atlantic colonies were not an improvisation. They were an old European practice— exported.

English settlers documented agreements obsessively. They reduced conversations to written deeds, recorded boundaries in fixed lines, and treated transactions as permanent transfers. Land, once "purchased," was assumed to be owned forever. English law recognized no obligation to revisit or renegotiate once the ink dried on a page.

Indigenous leaders understood these arrangements very differently. Land was not an inert possession to be alienated permanently. It was a shared resource governed by use, season, and necessity. Agreements granting access were conditional, bounded by behavior and circumstance. If conditions changed, the agreement could change accordingly. This was not bad faith. It was governance.

The imbalance lay not only in power, but in permanence.

As English settlements stabilized, dependence quietly shifted direction. Colonists no longer relied as heavily on Indigenous food or guidance. New ships arrived. Populations increased. What had begun as fragile outposts became self-sustaining towns. At the same time, Indigenous leaders found that the newcomers' expectations did not retreat as conditions changed. Access became entitlement. Presence became possession.

What had once been negotiated coexistence hardened into assumption. English courts enforced agreements that Indigenous leaders had never understood as final. Fences appeared where seasonal movement had once been expected. Disputes were redirected away from Indigenous councils and into colonial legal systems that recognized only one side's claims.

The assistance that had saved the colonies was not forgotten—but it was no longer honored. By the time Indigenous leaders realized that accommodation was being reinterpreted as submission, the balance had already shifted. The English no longer needed to ask for permission to survive. They believed they had acquired the right to remain.

This was the quiet turning point in early American history. Not conquest by force alone, but survival converted into entitlement—made possible by Indigenous restraint, knowledge, and diplomacy, and then used to erase the conditions under which that survival had been granted. This fundamental misunderstanding would define the region's future.

Shifting Alliances and Rising Tension

As the English settlements expanded, Indigenous nations were forced into increasingly difficult choices. Some leaders sought accommodation, hoping to preserve autonomy through alliance and restraint. Others viewed resistance as necessary to halt encroachment. Many attempted both, adjusting strategy as conditions changed.

Lieutenant. Lion Gardiner (and his forces) attacked by "Pequot" Indians at Saybrook Fort, 22 Feb 1637 (Pequot war). Watercolor on paper. Public Domain.

Colonial authorities exploited existing rivalries. Alliances were encouraged selectively, rewarding some nations while isolating others. The result was not peace, but fragmentation. Traditional mechanisms for resolving disputes were undermined as English courts, laws, and military power intruded into Indigenous governance. The Pequot War of the 1630s marked a turning point. English colonists, aided by Native allies, destroyed Pequot power through a campaign of violence that shattered any remaining illusion of coexistence on equal terms. The war demonstrated that English settlements would respond to resistance with overwhelming force—and that alliance with the English did not guarantee long-term security.

Leadership Under Constraint

Indigenous Leadership in Southern New England during this period was shaped by shrinking options. Sachems were responsible not only for defending territory but also for preventing annihilation. Decisions were made amid disease, military imbalance, and relentless land pressure.

Colonial records often portray Indigenous leaders as inconsistent or unreliable, particularly when agreements were challenged or revoked. In reality, leaders were responding to conditions that changed faster than any treaty could address. Agreements made under one set of circumstances became untenable under another.

The biographies that follow illustrate these pressures from different angles. Some leaders believed accommodation offered the best chance of survival. Others concluded that resistance was unavoidable. All operated within a system increasingly tilted against them.

The End of Balance

By the mid-seventeenth century, the political equilibrium that had defined Southern New England for generations was gone. English settlements expanded inland. Indigenous autonomy contracted. Warfare escalated. What began as cautious coexistence hardened into conflict. The region would soon be engulfed in one of the most destructive wars in colonial history. The decisions that led there—alliances formed, warnings ignored, compromises attempted—were shaped by the conditions described in this chapter.

Southern New England was not lost because its leaders failed to act. It was lost because the system they confronted did not allow for mutual restraint.

[1] Neal Salisbury, Manitou and Providence: Indians, Europeans, and the Making of New England, 1500–1643 (New York: Oxford University Press, 1982), 102–110.

Massasoit

Sachem, Wampanoag Confederacy

1581 – 1661

Chapter 5 — Massasoit, Wampanoag Confederacy

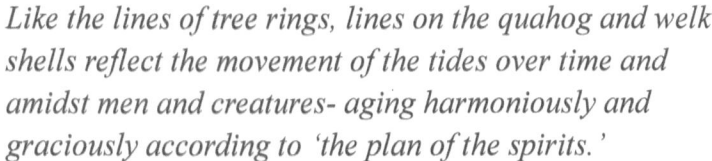

Like the lines of tree rings, lines on the quahog and welk shells reflect the movement of the tides over time and amidst men and creatures- aging harmoniously and graciously according to 'the plan of the spirits.'

— Ernestine Gray, Wampanoag

WHEN THE ENGLISH ESTABLISHED Plymouth in 1620, they entered a region already weakened by epidemic disease and destabilized by shifting power. The Wampanoag Confederacy, once dominant across southeastern New England, had suffered severe population loss in the years immediately preceding English settlement. Rival nations, particularly the Narragansett, remained comparatively strong. Within this altered balance, Massasoit rose to prominence.

A Confederacy Under Strain

The Wampanoag homeland encompassed present-day southeastern Massachusetts and parts of Rhode Island, including coastal plains, river valleys, and productive farmland. Before the epidemic collapse, the confederacy wielded significant influence through trade, diplomacy, and military strength. That influence eroded rapidly after disease decimated villages and disrupted leadership succession.

By the time the English arrived, the Wampanoag faced a reduced population, internal strain, and external threats. The Narragansett, who had suffered fewer losses, posed a real danger. English settlers, though few in number, were a new and unpredictable factor—one that could either intensify existing threats or be leveraged to counter them.

The Wampanoag would depend on a leader who could guide them through this time of transition, and his choices would forever change the landscape of North America. That man was Massasoit.

Born around 1581 in what would one day be called Rhode Island, Massasoit was not his name at all but his title—great sachem—a term of authority rather than identity. The English, hearing the word and missing its meaning, treated it as a proper name, and in doing so fixed him in their records not as a man but as a role, a mistake that would follow him through history and into memory.

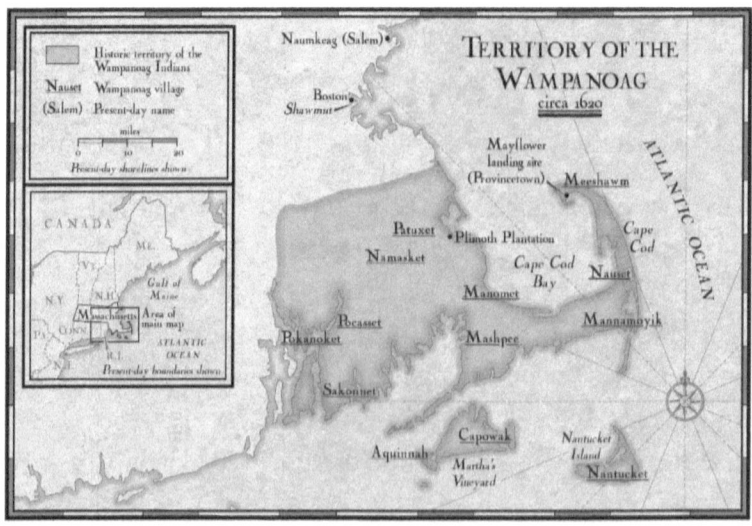

From the beginning, Massasoit acted with calculation rather than impulse. He neither rushed to confront the English newcomers nor ignored them. Before any formal meeting took place, he chose to observe, test, and measure the English through an intermediary.

That intermediary was Samoset.

Samoset was neither a Wampanoag sachem nor a figure of great political importance in the region. He was an Abenaki sagamore from the Muscongus Bay area of what is now Maine, a coastal region long exposed to European fishermen and traders. Through repeated contact with crews working the northern waters, Samoset had learned some English—a rare and valuable skill. He was familiar enough with Europeans to approach them without immediate fear, yet distant enough from Massasoit's inner circle that his loss, if the encounter turned violent, would not destabilize the confederacy.

Sending Samoset was deliberate. If the English were hostile, impulsive, or desperate, they would reveal themselves quickly. If they were cautious, weakened, or open to negotiation, that would become clear as well. Massasoit risked little while learning much.

In March 1621, Samoset walked into the Plymouth settlement alone and found it on the brink of collapse.[1] The English had arrived late in the season, unprepared for the climate and terrain. Disease spread in cramped quarters, and food stores dwindled. The survivors were few, weakened, and isolated along a coastline they did not understand. Their "colony" was, at that point, a fragile camp that could be wiped out by hunger, exposure, or a single determined attack.

The colonists were startled when a Native man approached them openly and spoke in broken but recognizable English. His greeting was simple, direct, and unmistakable, cutting through months of fear and isolation. For the English, it was the first proof that communication, and therefore survival, might be possible.

Samoset did not arrive offering submission or friendship. He asked questions, assessed the settlement's condition, population, and leadership, and learned that the English were hungry, poorly supplied, and dependent on the coming spring. He also made clear that they were not alone—that powerful Native nations watched them closely and that their survival would depend on relationships they did not yet understand.

After spending the night, Samoset left as calmly as he had arrived. He returned to Massasoit with information rather than promises. The English were weak yet organized. They were frightened but not immediately aggressive. They wanted trade and protection. They expected permanence.

Only then did Massasoit move forward.

Alliance as Strategy

Massasoit faced a different crisis. His confederacy had been battered by epidemic disease, and the rival Narragansett remained a serious threat. The Wampanoag needed allies, access to trade, and time to recover. A small English settlement, though unimpressive in size, was a new variable: a potential trading partner, a potential military counterweight, and a potential threat if it grew.

When he chose to meet the English in person, he did so on his terms, at a time and place of his choosing, and with a clear understanding of who held the advantage in that moment. Samoset's mission confirmed what Massasoit suspected: the settlers needed allies more than land and could be approached without immediate danger.

This first contact set the pattern for what followed. It was not driven by curiosity or goodwill but by intelligence gathering, restraint, and strategy. Massasoit did not gamble his people's future on first impressions. He tested the newcomers, learned their weaknesses, and only then stepped forward to negotiate.

Massasoit smoking a ceremonial pipe with Governor John Carver in Plymouth, 1621, as imagined by a 19th-century engraver. Public domain.

The English would later remember this sequence as a moment of providence or welcome. In reality, it was a controlled encounter, carefully staged by an Indigenous leader who understood that survival in a changing Atlantic world depended on knowing when—and how—to engage.

Out of this convergence of weakness and calculation came the 1621 agreement forged between Massasoit and the Plymouth colonists. While it has often been portrayed as a moment of mutual trust or cultural exchange, in reality, it was a defensive alliance shaped by immediate necessity.

As recorded in English sources, the terms included mutual non-aggression, commitments to warn one another of threats, provisions for the return of stolen goods, and a promise of assistance if either party were attacked. It was not a celebration of shared values; it was a reactive pact to stabilize a volatile situation. In effect, it established a framework for coexistence and alliance: the English gained protection and the ability to survive long enough to become established, while Massasoit gained leverage in a shifting regional power struggle and an avenue for trade.

The alliance worked, at least temporarily, because each side needed the other. Plymouth needed food, local knowledge, and time. Massasoit needed a partner to deter rivals and supply goods increasingly valuable in an Atlantic economy. But the agreement was never equal, and it was never understood in the same way.

For Massasoit, such an arrangement fit within an Indigenous diplomatic tradition that assumed reciprocity, ongoing negotiation, and the possibility of revising terms as circumstances changed. The relationship was meant to be managed over time, not frozen permanently. For the English, recording the agreement on paper signaled a binding contract that could later be cited as proof of legitimacy, obedience, and—eventually—rights to land and jurisdiction. What began as a practical compact between vulnerable parties would, in English hands, become part of a growing archive of documents used to justify permanence.

That difference was the seed of future conflict. When Plymouth was weak, it acted as a partner. As it strengthened, it increasingly acted as an authority. The agreement did not fail because it was naïve. It failed because the balance of power that made it workable could not last, and because English concepts of fixed title and permanent jurisdiction were fundamentally incompatible with Indigenous expectations of conditional access and ongoing reciprocity.

Managing English Expansion

For several decades, Massasoit worked to maintain stability through restraint. He tolerated English settlement within limits, intervened to prevent conflict, and sought to manage disputes before they escalated. Massasoit forged relationships with colonial leaders, including William Bradford, Edward Winslow, Stephen Hopkins, John Carver, and Myles Standish.

His goal was to fold Plymouth into a wider Indigenous political landscape—one more actor to be managed, not a force destined to dominate.

That, however, required constant intervention. Disputes began almost immediately because the English settlement was inherently contentious. Livestock wandered into Native planting fields. Settlers cut timber and harvested resources beyond what Wampanoag leaders considered acceptable use. New arrivals pushed outward from the original settlement in search of arable land and freshwater. The English interpreted these moves as ordinary growth. Wampanoag communities experienced them as boundary violations. Massasoit's role was to prevent those violations from triggering retaliation that the English could then use to justify escalation.

He also had to manage the unpredictable behavior of the settlers themselves. Plymouth was not a monolith; it was a small, anxious society whose internal tensions often spilled outward. Individual colonists traded illegally, cheated in exchanges, or acted with arrogance, undermining fragile trust. Massasoit understood that one reckless act could spiral into violence, and that violence—once initiated—would not remain local. His leadership depended on seeing beyond the immediate insult to the larger consequences.

At the same time, he used diplomacy to keep channels open. Trade was not merely economic; it was political. Exchange created obligations, patterns of dependence, and opportunities for leverage. Massasoit maintained access to goods that strengthened his position within regional rivalries, while also keeping the English tied to an alliance they could not yet afford to abandon. This was not a passive peace. It was a negotiated peace, held together through continual recalibration.

Massasoit's restraint, however, did not mean passivity. It required vigilance, intelligence gathering, and timely intervention. One of the clearest examples occurred only a few years after Plymouth's founding, when English survival was still uncertain, and the regional balance remained volatile.

Wessagusset Affair

Massasoit learned of a plot by a group of Massachusett warriors to attack both the Plymouth settlement and the nearby English outpost at Wessagusset.[2] The plan was not irrational. Wessagusset, poorly governed and increasingly aggressive in its demands for food, had antagonized neighboring communities, and its collapse would have been readily justified under Indigenous norms of defense and reprisal. Plymouth, though less provocative, was vulnerable by proximity and association.

Massasoit understood the consequences. A coordinated attack would almost certainly eliminate the English presence in the region. It would also trigger retaliation— either from surviving settlers or from other English colonies already forming along the coast. What might begin as a local resolution could escalate into a broader conflict that would destabilize the entire southern New England balance.

He chose to intervene.

Rather than joining or quietly permitting the attack, Massasoit warned the English leadership in advance. The warning gave Plymouth time to respond, fortify, and act preemptively. The outcome—most famously the violent confrontation later remembered as the Wessagusset affair—was brutal and morally compromised, but from Massasoit's perspective, it prevented a larger and more uncontrollable war at a moment when his confederacy could not afford one.

This intervention was not an act of loyalty to the English. It was an act of regional management.

Massasoit and the English

Massasoit calculated that preserving the English settlements—contained, indebted, and still weak—was preferable to unleashing a cycle of violence that would invite further colonization and military response. By warning Plymouth, he asserted influence over events without committing his people to direct action. He also reinforced the alliance's utility: cooperation, when it served Indigenous interests, could avert catastrophe.

Later, English writers framed this episode as evidence of Massasoit's goodwill or gratitude. In reality, it was an example of disciplined leadership under constraint. He did not save the English because he trusted them. He saved them because their destruction at that moment would have produced consequences worse than their continued presence.

The episode illustrates the narrowness of the path Massasoit walked. Every decision required weighing immediate advantage against long-term survival. The warning to Plymouth was not a turning point because it preserved peace. It was a turning point because it revealed how fragile that peace already was—and how much effort was required to maintain it.

But the conditions that made restraint viable did not remain stable. Plymouth did not stay small. New settlements emerged, sometimes under Plymouth's authority, sometimes nearby and independent. As English numbers increased, the colonists' dependence on Native food and guidance decreased. As that dependence waned, so did humility. The alliance began to shift from a relationship between parties that both needed restraint to one in which one party increasingly believed it could impose terms.

This was the danger Massasoit could not fully control: demographic momentum. An agreement might regulate behavior, but it could not slow ships crossing the Atlantic, prevent land hunger, or stop the transformation of negotiated access into permanent occupation. Each year that Plymouth survived made the next year harder for the Wampanoag, as English survival was converted into entitlement—first to remain, then to expand, then to govern.

Massasoit's restraint bought time, and time mattered. It delayed war, protected communities during a period of recovery, and kept regional instability from erupting into open conflict. Massasoit's diplomacy could manage incidents. It could not reverse a system built for expansion.

The Calculus of Survival

Massasoit's role in early colonial New England was foundational in the plainest sense: without his diplomacy, Plymouth likely would not have survived long enough to become permanent. The 1621 treaty did more than prevent immediate violence. It stabilized a fragile settlement at the precise moment it was weakest, gave it access to food and trade, and—just as importantly—gave it time.

Time became Plymouth's decisive weapon. As ships arrived and populations grew, the colony's initial dependence on Indigenous aid transformed into self-sufficiency, and self-sufficiency into expansion. In that way, Massasoit helped create the conditions under which English colonization could become irreversible—even though preventing dispossession was never his goal, and could never have been achieved by goodwill alone.

Massasoit's leadership is often remembered for this early cooperation. That memory, shaped largely by colonial narratives, obscures the reality of his position. Accommodation was not an act of goodwill. It was a strategic calculation under pressure, a difficult compromise in a moment when survival required it. The alliance was not "friendship." It was statecraft under constraint and one of the earliest political foundations of what would later become the United States.

For Indigenous peoples of Southern New England, Massasoit's leadership represented something more complicated and more tragic: an attempt to contain an expanding system by treating it like a manageable neighbor rather than an unstoppable force. For roughly half a century, he maintained a working peace through constant negotiation, strategic restraint, and—at moments—direct intervention to prevent wider war. English sources describe him as reliable and peace-minded, and they preserve episodes in which he warned Plymouth of threats and counseled caution.

But even a gifted diplomat could not hold back demographic momentum. The longer the peace lasted, the more it favored the colony's growth; and the more it grew, the less it needed to honor the reciprocal logic that had made peace possible in the first place.

The collapse came quickly after Massasoit's death, traditionally dated to about 1661, though some accounts place it slightly earlier or later. His son Wamsutta (Alexander) inherited a far harsher reality and moved toward new political alignments, including closer ties with neighboring English colonies. Within a few years, Wamsutta was dead, and his brother Metacom (Philip) would lead the Wampanoag into the conflict that later English histories would call King Philip's War—a war that shattered Indigenous autonomy across much of the region.

In retrospect, Massasoit appears an unlikely founding father: not because he intended to found anything English, but because his success in keeping the peace allowed the colonial project to survive its vulnerable infancy. For his own people and their neighbors, that same peace postponed immediate catastrophe but could not prevent the larger one.

[1] Winslow, Edward; William Bradford (1865) [1622]. Henry Martyn Dexter (ed.). Mourt's Relation or Journal of the Plantation at Plymouth. Boston: John Kimball Wiggin

[2] William Bradford, Of Plymouth Plantation, 1620–1647, ed. Samuel Eliot Morison (New York: Alfred A. Knopf, 1952), 201–206.

Metacom
Sachem, Pokanoket, Wampanoag Confederacy
1638 – August 12, 1676

Wamsutta
Sachem, Pokanoket, Wampanoag Confederacy
1634 – 1662

Chapter 6 — The Sons of Massasoit: Inheriting a Peace That Could Not Last

We belong to the land, not the land to us.

— Native American Proverb

WHEN MASSASOIT DIED IN the early 1660s, he left behind more than a confederacy. He left a strategy—one that relied on restraint, reciprocity, and a balance of power that had already disappeared. His sons inherited not the conditions that had made diplomacy workable but the consequences of its success.

The English colonies that Massasoit had helped stabilize were no longer fragile. They were expanding, confident, and increasingly impatient with Indigenous autonomy. The coast was now a lattice of towns and jurisdictions. The Massachusetts colony now included the towns of Boston, Charlestown, Cambridge, and Salem. Along the Connecticut River and Long Island Sound corridor lie Hartford, Windsor, and Wethersfield. All told, roughly twenty thousand English inhabitants were now occupying the very river valleys and coastal plains that had once been negotiated through reciprocity and seasonal use.[1]

English livestock trampled planting fields, fences hardened boundaries, and courts converted conditional agreements into permanent title. Towns founded in the 1630s and 1640s were no longer experiments; they were entrenched communities with roads, militias, and expanding claims.

What had once been an alliance now felt, to colonial authorities, like entitlement.

Wamsutta was the first to confront that reality.

Wamsutta: The End of Deference

Known to the English as Alexander, Wamsutta assumed leadership of the Wampanoag in a world that was fundamentally different from the one his father had navigated. The balance of power had shifted. The English were confident, growing in number, and expanding rapidly.

Born around 1634, he was Massasoit's eldest son and, after his father's death, assumed leadership of the Pokanoket, a Wampanoag tribe in Massachusetts and Rhode Island. Sometime afterward, Wamsutta and his younger brother, Metacom, traveled to Plymouth to appear before the colonial court. Such a visit was not, in itself, unusual. Wampanoag custom marked significant moments—deaths, transitions of authority, shifts in responsibility—by adopting new names. Names were not fixed; they were earned, adapted, and sometimes discarded as circumstances changed.

What was unusual was where the brothers went to make that change. Instead of announcing their new names within their own councils, Wamsutta and Metacom stood before English magistrates and asked to be formally and publicly known by English names. The request was granted. Wamsutta became Alexander. Metacom became Philip.

To the Plymouth court, the moment likely seemed benign—perhaps even reassuring. Two Native leaders, voluntarily submitting their identities to English record books, accepted names that fit neatly within colonial custom. It could be read as cooperation, even assimilation.

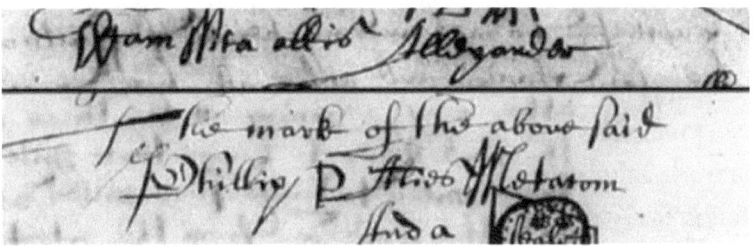

The mark of Wamsutta and Metacom with their English names in a court document.

For the Wampanoag, the meaning was more complex.

The adoption of English names did not signal surrender of authority. It was a political accommodation, an acknowledgment that English power now mattered in ways it had not before. By allowing their names to be entered in colonial records, the brothers were navigating a world in which English courts increasingly claimed jurisdiction over Native affairs. The act was not so much a submission as a recognition of a shifting balance.

But once written down, names became fixed—attached to deeds, treaties, summonses, and accusations. What had been a flexible marker of life stages hardened into an identity the courts could claim to define. Alexander and Philip would soon learn what their father had already begun to suspect: that appearing before English authority, even on one's own terms, carried consequences that could not be undone. The act of naming, intended to mark continuity after Massasoit's death, instead marked the narrowing space in which his sons would be allowed to rule.

Wamsutta's strategy in those initial months was quiet yet firm resistance. He sought new alliances, including closer ties with the Connecticut Colony, which Plymouth leadership saw as defiance. In 1662, Wamsutta was seized while traveling near Plymouth and brought before colonial officials. He was accused of planning an attack with the Narragansetts and of negotiating land sales without authorization. He was pressured and released only after he fell gravely ill. He died shortly afterward. While his cause of death remains unclear, his brother Metacomet, who succeeded him, held the belief that he had been poisoned. English sources denied this wrongdoing, but Indigenous communities did not forget the events.

THE DEATH OF ALEXANDER.

By Harper's Magazine - Page 29 June, 1857. Public Domain.

Wamsutta's death shattered any remaining illusion that the alliance forged by Massasoit still operated on reciprocal terms. Leadership had passed, but respect had not.

Metacom: When Containment Failed

Metacom, known as King Philip to the English, inherited power in the shadow of his brother's death and in a landscape where accommodation no longer slowed expansion—it enabled it. English settlements continued to press deeper into Wampanoag territory. Courts asserted more authority. Mission towns divided communities, arms were confiscated, and colonial surveillance increased.

Metacom understood what his father had hoped to avoid: peace, under these conditions, was no longer neutral. It favored the colonists exclusively.

Metacom was born around 1638, the second son of Massasoit. He served as sachem of the Wampanoag people from 1662 to 1676. In the years before the conflict, he urged restraint and sought to delay confrontation. He negotiated. He signed agreements under duress. He complied publicly while preparing privately. English authorities interpreted each concession as proof that pressure worked.

Philip himself moved with ease between worlds. For him, the world had always included colonists as integral members of the community; he knew no different. He wore finely worked English lace and richly detailed wampum belts, symbols of status and diplomacy among his own people. Unlike most Wampanoag, he kept pigs — an unmistakable sign of adaptation to the colonial economy. Among his close companions were both Englishmen and Native leaders. He was known to travel frequently to Boston, where he conducted business, met officials, and walked the busy streets with confidence. He was as comfortable negotiating in colonial towns as he was moving through the forests and coastal settlements of his homeland. But this balance was becoming harder to maintain.

By the early 1670s, Metacom understood the pressures closing in on his people did not come from a single direction. They arrived in waves, each reinforcing the next. Along the coast, English settlements continued to spread outward from their original footholds. Fields expanded, and hunting grounds shrank. The game became scarce not because the land had failed, but because it had been claimed and repurposed.

What English farmers called 'improvement,' Indigenous communities experienced as the erosion of territory, food security, and autonomy. As English settlers pushed deeper into Native territory, Philip attempted to slow the tide. He declared a moratorium on further land sales, hoping to preserve what remained of Wampanoag autonomy. But settlement continued. Trust evaporated. Each year brought new encroachments, new disputes, and fewer avenues for redress. Metacom delayed confrontation as long as he could, but delay no longer slowed the process. The system he faced did not require provocation to expand.

Yet he continued to speak for peace even as younger warriors grew increasingly angry at the steady encroachment of English settlement. To many of Philip's followers, patience began to feel like surrender.

Colonial authorities showed little interest in compromise.

Metacom responded as he always had: through alliance. He worked to knit together a network of Native nations bound by shared grievance rather than shared culture. Some had lost land; others had lost leverage; many had lost patience. The goal was not conquest but reversal—the hope that coordinated resistance might still push the English back toward the coast, or at least halt their advance. But events beyond Southern New England were already shaping the outcome.

Meanwhile, tensions within Native communities continued to rise. Warriors demanded action. Raids began. The Narragansett soon joined the widening conflict. Towns were attacked and property destroyed as the war spread rapidly across Rhode Island, Connecticut, and into eastern New York. More tribes entered the struggle as violence escalated. To the west, the Haudenosaunee Confederacy was engaged in a brutal series of skirmishes later known as the Beaver Wars. Armed through the fur trade and determined to control access to European markets, the Iroquois pushed rival nations east and south. Displacement rippled outward, compressing populations and intensifying competition for land and resources. The pressure that seemed local was, in fact, continental.

Metacom's territory lay between forces he could not command.

Colonists fled isolated settlements and sought safety behind the defenses of larger towns. Some abandoned New England entirely and returned to England. What had begun as a regional dispute was becoming a full-scale frontier war. Philip had tried to hold the line between accommodation and resistance. But now events were slipping beyond any one leader's control.

In 1671, Plymouth's leaders made that reality explicit. Metacom was summoned before the colonial authorities and compelled to accept terms that stripped away what little independence he had left. He was required to surrender much of his people's arms and ammunition—an act that left the Wampanoag exposed as violence was already spreading across the region. He was also forced to acknowledge subjection to English law, a declaration that recast a sovereign leader as a regulated subject. To Philip and many of his followers, this felt less like diplomacy and more like deliberate humiliation — a calculated attempt to provoke submission.

War Without Illusion

Phillip's final decision to start an open war came after a period of widespread complaint, inequality, and force. By then, there were no other options. It was the culmination of a decade of tightening control.

King Philip's War was among the most destructive conflicts in colonial American history. It engulfed Southern New

England, devastated towns, and shattered Indigenous autonomy throughout the region. Metacom forged alliances across tribal lines, drawing in leaders who had once hoped that accommodation might preserve their people.

The colonies' response was overwhelming. Roughly a thousand militia, reinforced by about one hundred and fifty Native allies, were assembled not for negotiation but for annihilation. In November 1675, Governor Josiah Winslow set the fighting force in motion against the Narragansett homeland. What followed was not a single battle but a campaign: villages burned in sequence, food stores destroyed, families driven into winter swamps, the logic of total war applied to a people not yet openly at war with the English.

The war ground on with relentless brutality. Roughly two thousand English colonists died during the conflict — a staggering loss for the small and fragile New England population.

But the balance of power was already shifting.

The English had long cultivated the Mohawks as useful allies on the northern frontier. When war came, that alliance proved devastating to Phillip. Mohawk warriors struck with ferocity, killing hundreds of Philip's men and destroying Native settlements in swift, punishing raids. Entire villages were burned. In some places, thousands of Native people were left dead in the wake of the violence.

Those who survived often faced a different fate. Hundreds were captured, marched to coastal ports, and shipped across the Atlantic. In the West Indies, they were sold into slavery

— men, women, and children severed forever from their homelands. By the war's later stages, many of the tribes aligned with Philip had been effectively crushed, their political and military power shattered.

The conflict soon reached Philip's own family. His nine-year-old son was arrested by colonial authorities and jailed. Despite his age, he was eventually transported overseas and sold into slavery in the Caribbean. It was a decision that shocked even some contemporaries, yet it reflected the hardening colonial resolve to eliminate any future threat.

At the same time, converted Native people living in the so-called "praying towns" faced growing suspicion. Many were forcibly removed from their homes. In the depths of winter, men, women, and children were driven to Deer Island in Boston Harbor. With little shelter, few blankets, and almost no provisions, several hundred died from exposure and disease.[2]

The campaign reached its bloody climax in the frozen wetlands of Rhode Island at what came to be called the Great Swamp Fight. The Narragansetts' main fort was surrounded, stormed, and set ablaze. Hundreds were killed—men, women, and children—many burned alive or cut down as they fled. The survivors regrouped under the sachem Canonchet and carried the war outward, striking back at the edges of the English world. Towns fell in flames as Native war parties pushed into Massachusetts Bay, Plymouth, and Rhode Island, destroying settlements and burning Providence to the ground in March 1676.

By the end, both Native and colonial societies had been permanently transformed. The land itself bore the scars of a war that had begun as a struggle for autonomy and survival, and ended as one of the most devastating conflicts in early American history. The Wampanoag and their Narragansett allies were shattered—not merely defeated, but broken as coherent peoples in southern New England. What remained were remnants: captives, refugees, and the enslaved. Entire communities were displaced or erased. The war ended not with negotiation but with annihilation and exile.

Metacom was killed in 1676. His body was mutilated, and his head was displayed—a message not only to surviving Indigenous peoples but also to future generations. The era of negotiated coexistence in Southern New England was over.

Native Americans attack a settlement during King Phillips War: North Wind Picture Archives Public Domain.

A Generational Reckoning

Together, Wamsutta and Metacom represent the closing of a door that Massasoit had worked to keep open. Their lives mark the transition from diplomacy to domination, from alliance to enforcement.

Philip, King of Mount Hope, from Benjamin Church's The Entertaining History of King Philip's War, line engraving, colored by hand by Paul Revere, 1772. Public Domain.

Massasoit's strategy was not naïve. It was rational for its time. But it relied on an assumption that English expansion could be contained by agreement. His sons learned, at great cost, that expansion was not a policy—it was a system.

Wamsutta's death revealed that Indigenous sovereignty would no longer be respected even in form. Metacom's war revealed that resistance, once necessary, would be met with eradication. In that sense, the sons of Massasoit were not failures. They were witnesses. Their leadership exposed the limits of accommodation and the price of resisting too late.

With their defeat, Southern New England ceased to be a contested Indigenous homeland and became a colonial possession. The strategies that had once preserved peace were no longer available to the leaders who followed.

Our story now turns north and inland to a different political world—one where power was wielded far from the coast and where Indigenous confederacy still constrained colonial ambition for another generation.

[1]"Estimated Population of American Colonies: 1610 to 1780 (HS/US vol. 2, p. 1168)," Vancouver Island University (transcription of Historical Statistics of the United States table

[2] Lepore, Jill (1998). The name of war : King Philip's War and the origins of American identity (1st ed.). New York.

Canochet

Sachem, Narragansett

c. 1635 - April 3, 1676

Chapter 7 —Canonchet, Narragansett

I Will Not Betray My People

—Canonchet

CANONCHET INHERITED A WORLD already tilting toward collapse. By the time he rose to leadership among the Narragansett, the balance of southern New England had shifted decisively. English towns pressed outward from the coast. Forest paths became survey lines. Seasonal movement hardened into permanent exclusion. Canonchet did not preside over first contact. He presided over the reckoning that followed.

The Narragansett homeland lay in what is present-day Rhode Island, centered around the broad saltwater bay that still carries their name. Their world was coastal and riverine—tidal inlets, marshes, oak forests, and sheltered coves that provided fish, shellfish, waterfowl, and access to maritime trade. Villages and planting grounds were organized around seasonal rhythms, with cornfields, fishing places, and travel routes woven into a landscape that was actively managed rather than merely inhabited.

Before English settlement became dominant, the Narragansett were among the most influential powers in southern New England. Epidemic disease struck the region unevenly, and the Narragansett suffered less than some nearby nations in the years just before Plymouth's founding—making them a formidable counterweight in the decades that followed. They contended with rivals such as the Mohegans and Pequots, navigated shifting alliances, and early recognized that Europeans could be used as leverage in Indigenous rivalries—until that leverage became dependency and dependency became control.

By the time Canonchet inherited leadership, the Narragansett were still powerful, but their power was now constrained by a tightening vise: English towns expanding from Massachusetts and Connecticut and a new political reality in which Indigenous sovereignty could be acknowledged one year and denied the next.

Narragansett Bay Map

Canonchet grew up in the long shadow of his father's death. Miantonomo, the most powerful Narragansett leader of his generation, was captured in 1643 after being defeated by the Mohegans, longtime rivals whose fortunes were rising through an alliance with the English. Rather than being treated as a defeated enemy subject to negotiation or ransom, Miantonomo was delivered into colonial custody, where English authorities faced an uncomfortable decision. They wished neither to execute him themselves nor to release a leader whose influence they feared.

The solution they devised laid bare the nature of colonial justice as clearly as any battlefield outcome. English officials consulted clergy, sought legal justification, and ultimately arranged for Miantonomo's execution by his Indigenous enemies, thereby preserving the appearance of neutrality while ensuring the result. He was led into the woods near Norwich, Connecticut, and killed by a Mohegan escort.[1] His death was not the outcome of a trial in any meaningful sense but rather the calculated removal of a political obstacle.

For the Narragansett, the message was unmistakable. Power no longer shielded a leader from elimination. Alliances did not guarantee restraint. English authority could determine outcomes while denying responsibility for them. Miantonomo's execution marked a turning point in southern New England, when Indigenous sovereignty ceased to be acknowledged, even in defeat.

Canonchet inherited more than leadership from his father. He inherited the lesson that accommodation had limits— and that those limits were defined not by treaties or mutual understanding but by colonial convenience. Miantonomo had tried to navigate the shifting balance of power through diplomacy and force in equal measure. His death taught Canonchet that the English would tolerate neither approach once a leader became inconvenient. That death lingered like an unpaid debt.

English colonies had learned to exploit Indigenous rivalries, elevating some leaders while isolating others. Canonchet watched Uncas and the Mohegans prosper through alliance, while older power structures were labeled threats and dismantled. Where Massasoit had once managed coexistence through careful accommodation, Canonchet came of age knowing that accommodation would only delay, not stop, expansion.

Canonchet

When war finally came in the 1670s, Canonchet did not rush toward it. He measured the moment carefully. King Philip's War was not a single uprising but a cascade of collapsing arrangements, and Canonchet understood that once the Narragansett committed themselves, there would be no retreat. The English demanded neutrality, but neutrality itself had become a trap. To remain still was to be surrounded.

The Great Swamp Fight in December 1675 shattered any remaining illusion that restraint would be rewarded. English forces, joined by colonial allies, attacked a fortified Narragansett winter village deep in the swamp. Hundreds were killed—many of them women, children, and elders. Villages burned. Food stores were destroyed. Survival itself became resistance. Canonchet emerged from the ruins not as a negotiator but as a leader of a people with nothing left to bargain with.

Captured in 1676, Canonchet was brought before colonial authorities who expected submission, confession, or useful intelligence. He offered none. When pressed to betray allies or accept mercy in exchange for cooperation, he refused. According to contemporary accounts, he declared that he would neither speak ill of other leaders nor purchase his life at the cost of his people.[2]

Canonchet's refusal to submit placed him squarely in the crosshairs of colonial authority. To English leaders, he challenged the premise that Native power could be neutralized by alliance, intimidation, or selective accommodation. His insistence on independence made him dangerous in ways that could not be resolved through treaty or negotiation.

The decision to execute him exposed the cold calculus of colonial justice. English officials resolved that Canonchet should not be killed by their own hands. Instead, they arranged for his death to be carried out by Native executioners—Pequot, Mohegan, and Niantic men drawn from nations already entangled in English alliance networks. The logic was explicit. Increase Mather later explained that forcing Indigenous enemies to kill Canonchet would render them "abominable to the other Indians," binding them permanently to English interests. It was an act designed not merely to eliminate a leader but to fracture Indigenous solidarity beyond repair.

Yet the English still offered him a final bargain. His life would be spared if he agreed to make peace and submit. Canonchet again refused. When told he would be executed, he responded without hesitation. He welcomed death, saying: "I like it well. I shall die before my heart is soft, and before I have spoken a word unworthy of myself." It was not bravado. It was a declaration.

In a final gesture heavy with meaning, Canonchet asked for his execution to be carried out by Uncas, the Mohegan sachem. He referred to Uncas as his "fellow prince"—both sons of chiefs, both leaders shaped by the same world, now standing on opposite sides of it. The request was denied or ignored. Instead, his execution was carried out by Oneco, Uncas's son, alongside the Pequot warrior Robin Cassacinamon and a Niantic sachem.[3] The symbolism was deliberate: former rivals made instruments of colonial order.

He was shot, drawn, and quartered at Stonington, Connecticut, on April 3, 1676, and treated as a traitor rather than an enemy leader. His head was sent to Hartford, where colonial officials proclaimed his death a victory. For them, Canonchet's execution signaled the collapse of Narragansett resistance. For Indigenous communities across New England, it confirmed something far more enduring—that English justice would extend as far as it needed to and that survival would increasingly depend on choosing sides in a war not of their making.

Canonchet's death marked not only the end of a war leader but also the end of the Narragansett as an independent power in southern New England. Survivors were sold into slavery, scattered, or absorbed into other communities. Their land was divided and redistributed.

What remains today are place names layered over a dispersed people. The Narragansett homeland now includes towns and cities such as Narragansett, Charlestown, Westerly, Providence, and, across the border in southeastern Connecticut, Stonington and New London. These communities sit atop former villages, planting grounds, and travel corridors that once sustained one of southern New England's most powerful Indigenous nations. The landscape still bears quiet witness to a world that existed long before colonial boundaries hardened into permanence.

If Massasoit represented the fragile promise of coexistence and Metacom the desperation of resistance, Canonchet stands for something harder to categorize: refusal without illusion. He did not believe the English could be persuaded to stop. He did not believe survival lay in alliance. He believed only that some lines, once crossed, could not be uncrossed—and that dignity might still be preserved, even if victory was impossible.

In that sense, Canonchet was not a failed diplomat or a defeated general. He was a leader who recognized that the era of negotiation had ended, and who chose not to pretend otherwise.

[1] Connecticut General Court Records, 1643, quoted in Charles J. Hoadly, ed., Records of the Colony of Connecticut, vol. 1 (Hartford: Case, Lockwood & Brainard, 1850).

[2] Slade, M. B. C. (December 16, 1876). "Distinguished Indians". New England Journal of Education.

[3] American National Biography (New York: Oxford University Press, 1999)

Part III— Hudson Valley, Long Island, and the
Haudenosaunee Power Sphere

Chapter 8 —The Hudson Corridor: River, Trade, and Power

Earth teach me quiet... as the grasses are still with new light. Earth teach me suffering... as old stones suffer with memory. Earth teach me humility... as blossoms are humble with beginning.

—Native American Proverb

THE HUDSON RIVER WAS never a boundary. It was a corridor.

Long before Europeans arrived, the river and its tributaries connected the Atlantic coast to the continent's interior, carrying people, goods, news, and influence between worlds that outsiders would later treat as separate. Control of this corridor meant access—not only to land, but to trade routes, alliances, and political leverage that extended far beyond the shoreline.

When settlers entered the Hudson Valley in the early seventeenth century, they stepped into a landscape already governed by Indigenous law and shaped by Indigenous power. What they encountered here was not the fragmented sachemships of Southern New England, but a layered political world in which local communities operated under the shadow—and often the direction—of a dominant inland confederacy.

A River System, Not a Frontier

The Hudson Valley connected coastal Algonquian-speaking peoples with interior nations through a web of rivers, portage routes, and seasonal travel.

In the Lower Hudson and Westchester, communities such as the Wappinger—including the Wecquaesgeek, Sinsink, Siwanoy, Wiechquaesgeek, Tappan, and Waoranecks— occupied a landscape dense with villages, trails, and planting grounds. These were river people in the fullest sense: their authority rested on access to crossings, fisheries, and the narrow points where traffic could be watched and taxed. They were close enough to the sea to encounter Europeans early and close enough to the interior to feel Haudenosaunee pressure constantly. Survival here meant flexibility—shifting alliances, strategic hospitality, calculated resistance—and an acute awareness that violence could arrive from either direction with little warning.

Farther north, in the Hudson Highlands and Mid-Hudson, groups such as the Esopus, Haverstraw (Rumachenanck), Kitchawank, and Minisink lived among steep ridges and narrow river corridors, where geography itself enforced caution. These communities controlled chokepoints— places where the river tightened, where portage routes mattered, and where a single misjudged move could cut off trade or invite reprisal. The Esopus, in particular, would learn how quickly Dutch trading relationships could harden into open war when land hunger replaced barter. Here, diplomacy was conducted with one eye on the river and the other on the forest beyond.

At the river's mouth and along the islands and sandy reaches of New York City and Long Island, a different rhythm prevailed. The Canarsie, Montaukett, Shinnecock, and Unquachog (Poospatuck) were oriented toward salt water as much as fresh—toward fishing grounds, shell banks, and seasonal movement along the coast. Their proximity to European ships brought early trade and early disruption, but it also placed them at the intersection of empires. Wampum flowed through these communities, as did information. What happened in the interior rarely stayed there; it arrived by canoe, by rumor, by refugee.

Along the New Jersey–New York harbor edge, groups such as the Hackensack occupied a liminal zone—politically tied to both the Mid-Atlantic and the Hudson Valley. They felt the pull of Lenape kinship to the south and the gravitational force of Haudenosaunee power to the north and west, while navigating Dutch and later English demands for land and loyalty.

The Hudson Bay was a convergence zone—where river-based trade became leverage, Dutch and English competition amplified Native rivalries, and the Haudenosaunee shadow loomed over every treaty, skirmish, and decision about whether to welcome the next ship or burn its outpost before it could take root. Their choices reverberated inland and reshaped the coast. European observers often mistook this system for fragmentation. In reality, it was distributed governance— local autonomy within broader political influence.

MICMAC

MALISEET
PASSAMAQUODDY

MT. KATAHDIN

EASTERN
ABENAKI

WESTERN
ABENAKI

WESTERN
ABENAKI

Mahican

WAMPANOAG
NIPMUCK
NARRAGANSETT
PEQUOT
MONTAUK

NANTICOKE
PISCATAWAY

ATLANTIC
OCEAN

LAKE
CHAMPLAIN

POWHATAN

ROANOKE

The Haudenosaunee Sphere

Inland, the Haudenosaunee Confederacy—the Mohawk, Oneida, Onondaga, Cayuga, Seneca, and later the Tuscarora—had built the most formidable political alliance in northeastern North America. Their villages lay west and south of the river's upper reaches, but their influence extended far beyond their fields. Through warfare, diplomacy, and carefully managed terror, the Haudenosaunee reshaped the balance of power throughout the Hudson watershed. No coastal group made decisions without considering how those decisions would be read upriver. Their power did not depend on occupying the coast. It rested on controlling movement through the interior: trade routes, diplomatic channels, and the terms governing war or peace.

The Mohawk served as gatekeepers between the Atlantic world and the confederacy's heartland. Through them flowed goods, intelligence, and influence. An alliance with the Haudenosaunee could offer protection—or invite retaliation. This inland power shaped every European interaction in the region. No treaty, trade agreement, or settlement along the Hudson existed in isolation from Haudenosaunee interests.

Dutch Entry and Commercial Colonization

The Dutch were the first Europeans to recognize the Hudson's commercial value. In 1609, Henry Hudson's ship sailed up the river that would later carry his name, charting a waterway linking the Atlantic to the continent's interior. The river was not neutral ground; it was a shared artery, governed by custom, alliance, and restraint, and closely watched by those who had long understood its value before Europeans arrived.

Within a decade, Dutch traders followed, establishing posts to extract wealth through the fur trade rather than establish settlements. This approach aligned more closely with existing Indigenous economies, at least initially.

The Dutch formalized their presence in the 1620s, founding Fort Orange near present-day Albany and later New Amsterdam at the river's mouth. Trade flowed quickly—beaver pelts outward, metal goods and firearms inward—and with it came consequences no one fully controlled. The Dutch relied on Indigenous partners for access to the interior, and Indigenous leaders leveraged that dependence to negotiate advantage. For a time, the Hudson Valley became a zone of calculated exchange rather than conquest.

But trade brought consequences. Firearms intensified warfare, hardened rivalries, and made the river corridor more dangerous even as it became more profitable. The demand for pelts reshaped hunting practices and strained relations among neighboring nations. Dutch forts and trading posts, though limited in number, anchored a European presence that was not easily dislodged.

For Indigenous leaders, the Dutch represented both opportunity and danger. Trade could strengthen a community's position, but it could also destabilize long-standing balances and draw nations into conflicts driven by European markets rather than by Indigenous needs. Alliances were transactional rather than territorial.

By the time English power replaced Dutch authority later in the century, the Hudson had already been transformed—from a negotiated Indigenous world into a contested imperial one.

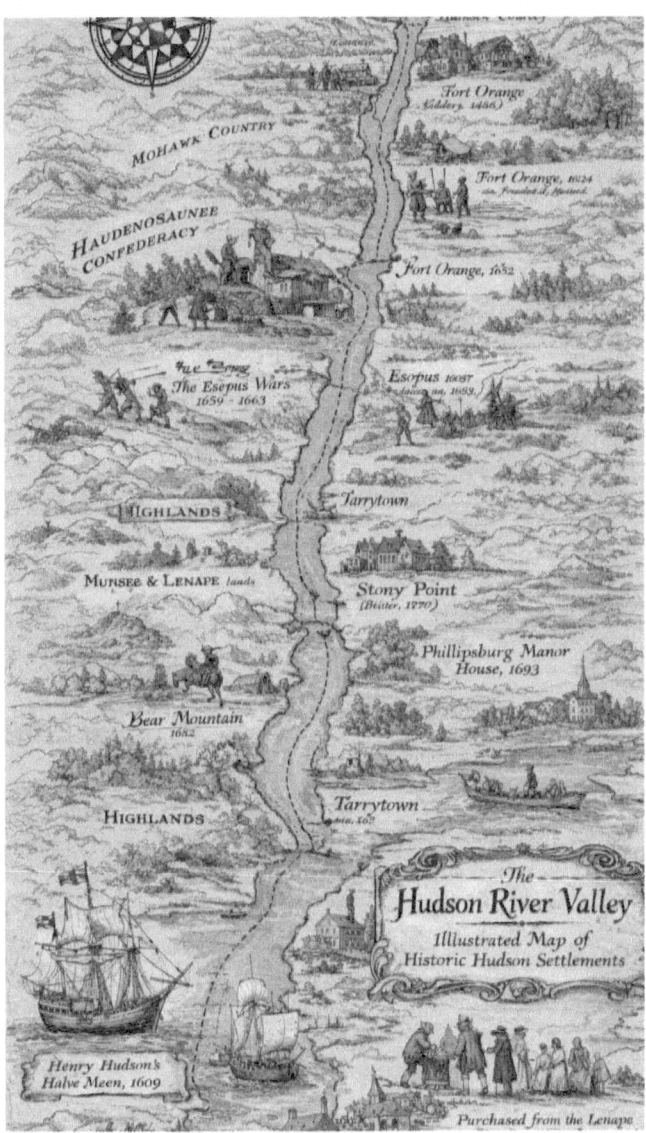

Hudson River Valley Map, Illustration

English Expansion and Escalation

When English power replaced Dutch authority in the mid-seventeenth century, the nature of colonization shifted. English settlements emphasized land ownership over trade dominance. Where the Dutch had sought access, the English sought control. Written deeds, surveyed boundaries, and permanent towns followed.

For Hudson Valley and Long Island nations, this shift proved disastrous. Agreements that had granted limited use or shared access were transformed into claims of exclusive ownership. English courts enforced documents that Indigenous leaders had never understood as final or irrevocable. Expansion accelerated, and restraint diminished.

Conflict followed.

The Hudson Valley's first sustained lesson in what "settlement" meant came not at Manhattan, but upriver at a place the Dutch called Wiltwijck—a small, anxious farming outpost on Esopus land near present-day Kingston.

The Esopus and the Cost of Standing in the Corridor

For the Indigenous nations of the Hudson Valley, geography was both an asset and a liability. The same river that connected them through trade and diplomacy also exposed them to colonizers seeking access to the interior. Among those caught in this corridor were the Esopus—Munsee-speaking Lenape whose villages and fields lined the fertile flats near present-day Kingston.

The Esopus lived where settlers wanted to stay.

Their villages and planting fields lay along one of the most fertile and strategically valuable stretches of the mid-Hudson Valley, precisely where Dutch trading posts evolved into permanent towns. As Wiltwijck—present-day Kingston—grew from a fortified outpost into an agricultural settlement, and Beverwyck—later Albany—expanded upriver, Esopus land was steadily absorbed into the colonial footprint.

This did not occur through a single decisive conquest, but through an accumulation of small intrusions: fenced fields pushed outward, livestock trampled cornfields, timber was cut beyond agreed limits, and settlers treated provisional arrangements as permanent rights. Each encroachment was small enough to be disputed, negotiated, or temporarily endured. Taken together, they overwhelmed diplomacy. By the time open conflict erupted, Esopus territory had already been hollowed out, its boundaries redrawn not only by war but also by the slow, relentless normalization of settlement.

The Esopus responded as leaders elsewhere had: through negotiation, warnings, and selective resistance. They understood that outright war risked annihilation and that unlimited accommodation invited erasure. The result was tension that flared repeatedly and violently.

The Esopus Wars of the 1650s and 1660s were not spontaneous outbursts. They were the product of years of unresolved conflict over land use, jurisdiction, and authority. Colonial officials treated Indigenous retaliation for lost land as criminal rather than defensive. Each side believed the other had violated an agreement the first side never fully recognized.

The first war erupted in 1659, when accumulated grievances boiled over into open fighting. Raids and counter-raids spread across the settlements. Farms were burned. Settlers clustered behind palisades, discovering too late what it meant to live as a small island of permanence in a world still moving by river and forest trail.

The second war, in 1663, was worse—sharper, more deceptive, and more damaging to any remaining trust. An attack on Wiltwijck came with the kind of timing and coordination colonists rarely anticipated, striking when people were dispersed and least ready. Captives were taken. Panic outran facts. The Dutch responded with punitive expeditions that treated villages as targets and the surrounding landscape as enemy territory.

Smaller conflicts were also frequent, localized, and brutal. Retaliation bred escalation. Communities were repeatedly relocated, moving inland, northward, or westward to escape pressure. Some sought protection through alliance with the Haudenosaunee; others attempted accommodation with colonial authorities. Few strategies succeeded for long.

What began as a local struggle over land use and authority became a template: settlement produced friction; friction produced violence; violence justified harsher control. By the time the fighting subsided, the Hudson corridor was no longer simply a trade river. It had become a war river—one in which the politics of property were enforced by palisades and gunpowder.

The Esopus did not disappear, but they were forced to adapt by relocating, dispersing, and surviving under constant pressure. Their leaders were not remembered for founding alliances or preserving peace. They are remembered for standing at the point where trade became settlement—and for learning, too late, that permanence was not negotiable.

The Mohawk: Gatekeepers of the Confederacy

As the easternmost nation of the Haudenosaunee Confederacy, the Mohawk served as its outward-facing shield and diplomatic voice to the Atlantic world. Goods moving inland passed through Mohawk hands, and so did information. Decisions made in Mohawk country shaped outcomes hundreds of miles away, including along the Hudson River and Long Island Sound.

The Haudenosaunee Confederacy was among the most sophisticated political systems in North America, built on balance rather than domination. Authority rested with councils, guided by clan mothers and constrained by consensus. Decisions on war and peace were not made by individuals but by a system designed to prevent fracture while projecting collective strength. This was misunderstood by the English, who sought out singular leaders, permanent treaties, and fixed allegiances. What they encountered instead was a confederacy that played the long game—adjusting alliances, exploiting rivalries between European powers, and maintaining autonomy well into the colonial era.

When Europeans arrived, the confederacy did not collapse under pressure. At first, it adapted. The Mohawk sought regulation. They negotiated from a position of strength, leveraging their geography and confederacy backing to set terms. This strategy placed them at the center of the Beaver Wars, a series of conflicts that reshaped the interior Northeast in the mid-seventeenth century. Armed through trade and driven by competition for hunting territory and access to European markets, the Haudenosaunee pushed rival nations outward. Displacement followed. Pressure rippled eastward, compressing populations toward the coast and into regions already strained by settlement.

A Region of Intermediaries

The Hudson corridor produced leaders who, by necessity, served as intermediaries. They negotiated among coastal and inland powers, European empires, and Indigenous nations with competing interests. Authority was fragile and constantly tested. A misjudged alliance could invite destruction, while refusing to engage could be equally dangerous. As in other places, European records often depict these leaders as inconsistent—friendly one year, hostile the next. In reality, they were responding to rapidly changing conditions in a system that lacked stable equilibrium once English settlement accelerated.

Setting the Stage

By the late seventeenth century, the Hudson Valley and Long Island had become among the most contested regions in eastern North America. Indigenous autonomy had not vanished, but it was under sustained pressure from all directions: colonial expansion, market-driven conflict, and the gravitational pull of inland power.

These leaders did not stop colonization. No single nation could. But they delayed it, redirected it, and forced

European powers to negotiate rather than dictate. In doing so, they showed that inland power could shape coastal outcomes—a lesson the English would learn repeatedly and never comfortably.

Hendrick Theyanoguin

Chief, Mohawk

c. 1691 – September 8, 1755

Chapter 9— Hendrick Theyanoguin: The Confederacy Speaks

We shall call each other Brother, as we are equal. In one canoe is our way of life, laws, and people. In the other is your ship with your laws, religion, and people. Our vessels will travel side by side down the river of life. Each will respect the ways of each other and will not interfere with the other, forever.

—Haudenosaunee, 1613

WHEN ENGLISH OFFICIALS SPOKE of Native "chiefs," they imagined men who ruled as they did— singular authorities, fixed in office, bound by hierarchy. The Haudenosaunee operated on an entirely different logic. Power did not reside in one man. It moved through councils, clans, and carefully maintained balance. Leaders spoke not for themselves, but for a system that restrained them as much as it empowered them.

Hendrick Theyanoguin emerged from that system.

By the time he entered English records in the early eighteenth century, the Mohawk had already spent more than a century managing European relations. They had negotiated with the Dutch, adapted to English rule, and navigated French pressure from the north. Hendrick did not invent Haudenosaunee diplomacy. He inherited it—

sharpened by generations of experience along the Hudson corridor.

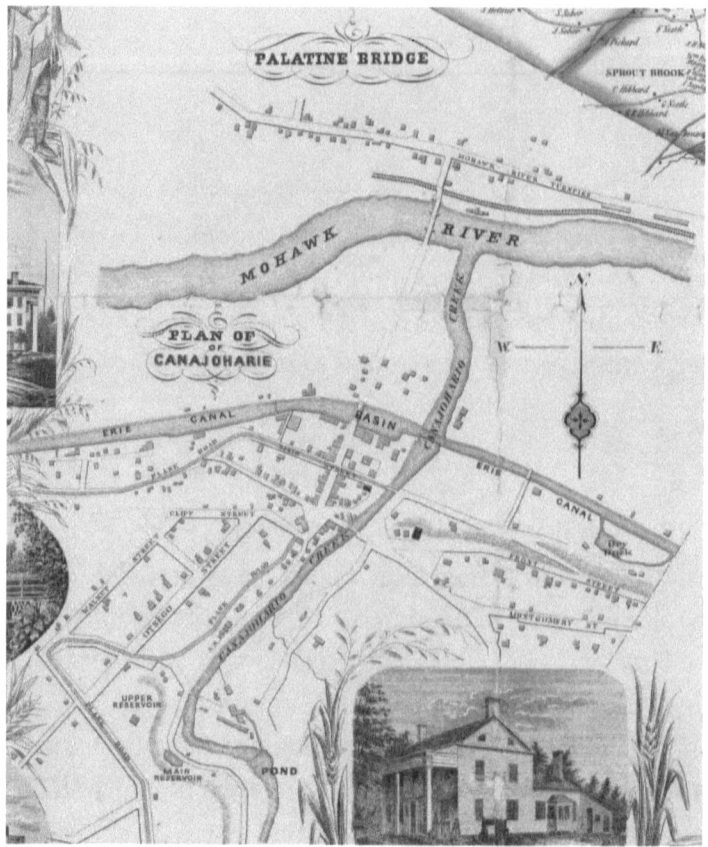

Canajoharie, Map

Theyanoguin was born around 1691 in Canajoharie, one of the two principal Mohawk communities on the south side of the Mohawk River. Europeans called it the Upper Castle, a term that revealed as much about their habits as about the place itself. To the Mohawk, it was neither an outpost nor a frontier but a center—anchored along a river that had long carried trade, diplomacy, and war between the interior and the coast. Upriver from Schenectady, Canajoharie stood at a point where power moved west as easily as it flowed east.

He rose within a political system that Europeans continually understood. He was a chief of the Bear Clan, one of the Mohawk's principal clans, and served in the Mohawk Council, where authority was collective and carefully constrained. Influence within the confederacy did not depend on title alone but on reputation, kinship, and the ability to speak for consensus rather than command it.

Mohawk society followed a matrilineal order that defied European expectations. Identity, property, and office passed through the mother's line. A man's authority was rooted not in his father but in his mother's clan, and it was her eldest brother—the maternal uncle—who played the dominant role in shaping his life. This system ensured continuity even in a world reshaped by war. Captives could be adopted, clans replenished, and losses absorbed without fracturing the whole. It was as much a political design as a social one.

Theyanoguin entered European records almost from birth. In 1692, he was baptized by the Dutch Reformed Church and given the name Hendrick, a gesture signaling early and sustained contact with colonial society. To the English, he would be called King Hendrick, a title that reflected their need to impose familiar hierarchies. He accepted the title, correcting them when it mattered and exploiting the misunderstanding when it helped.

But Mohawk did not crown kings. They cultivated spokesmen, negotiators, and guardians of balance. Hendrick Theyanoguin would become all three.

Theyanoguin's authority rested not on command but on articulation—his ability to make the confederacy's interests intelligible to outsiders who neither understood nor trusted collective power.

He spoke English fluently, dressed in European clothing when diplomacy required it, and understood colonial law well enough to expose its contradictions. He reminded governors that treaties were mutual obligations, not instruments of submission. He warned them—repeatedly— that land hunger, unchecked settlement, and broken promises would produce war.

They listened when it suited them. They ignored him when it did not.

Theyanoguin's speeches, preserved in colonial records, reveal a leader who understood the trajectory of empire better than many of the men negotiating with him. He knew English expansion was relentless, that alliances were temporary, and that Indigenous survival depended on leverage rather than trust. He pressed for limits on settlement and insisted on the confederacy's sovereignty. He invoked memory—agreements made, boundaries promised, words given and broken.

What made him dangerous, in English eyes, was not hostility but resilience. He represented a political order that had not collapsed under colonial pressure. The Haudenosaunee still controlled the interior. They still determined whether trade routes remained open and whether war would remain localized or expand. Hendrick's presence was a reminder that the coast did not define power and that English claims to dominance were incomplete.

Theyanoguin, Illustration

By the mid-1740s, Theyanoguin had become one of the most visible Indigenous diplomats in northeastern North America, a man who moved comfortably among councils and colonies, war paths and conference tables. In 1746, he led a delegation of Mohawk leaders north to Montreal to meet Charles de la Boische, Marquis de Beauharnois, governor of New France.[1] The conference was formal, ritualized, and wary—another attempt by competing empires to secure Haudenosaunee allegiance in a borderland already primed for war. Nothing decisive was settled. Alliances, as always, remained conditional.

On the return journey, diplomacy gave way to violence. Near Lake Champlain, the Mohawk party encountered a small group of Frenchmen gathering timber. One man was killed, another captured, and the delegation continued south toward Albany.[2] The incident was neither accidental nor anomalous. It reflected the region's uneasy reality, where diplomacy and war were not opposites but parallel tools, deployed as circumstances demanded.

That same spring, Theyanoguin led a war party north toward the St. Lawrence, probing French defenses near Montreal. The attack was repulsed, and French forces failed to capture him. Even then, he remained elusive, protected as much by reputation as by terrain.

When open war erupted with the outbreak of the French and Indian War, Theyanoguin aligned firmly with the British. In 1755, he led Mohawk warriors through the Hudson Valley toward Crown Point, where British forces hoped to halt French expansion. He understood the stakes. Control of the interior meant control of the river corridors that sustained both empires and threatened Haudenosaunee autonomy.

Theyanoguin did not live to see how the war would end. On September 8, 1755, at the Battle of Lake George, he was killed while trying to halt the advance of French forces. His horse was shot out from under him. As he rose, he was bayoneted.[3] He was in his sixties—an old man by the standards of a life spent in councils and campaigns—yet he died as he had lived, at the intersection of empire and Indigenous sovereignty. His death removed one of the last great Mohawk leaders capable of navigating both worlds with authority. The war would continue. The alliances would harden. And the space for diplomacy—already narrowing—would shrink even further.

In this sense, he stands for the Mohawk leaders who came before him and those who followed. He was not the first to speak for the confederacy, nor would he be the last. But he is the clearest voice we have—a leader whose words endured because they unsettled those who recorded them.

The Hudson Valley taught Europeans that power did not always announce itself with crowns. Authority could be collective, memory political, and restraint stronger than force—at least until numbers and empire overwhelmed balance.

[1] William N. Fenton, The Great Law and the Longhouse: A Political History of the Iroquois Confederacy (Norman: University of Oklahoma Press, 1998
[2] Ian K. Steele, Warpaths: Invasions of North America (New York: Oxford University Press, 1994)
[3] Fred Anderson, Crucible of War: The Seven Years' War and the Fate of Empire in British North America, 1754–1766 (New York: Alfred A. Knopf, 2000)

Wyandanch

Sachem, Montaukett

c. 1590– 1659

Chapter 10 — Wyandanch, Montaukett

One arrow can be easily broken. But when five arrows are
be bound together, they become strong.

— Peacemaker to the Mohawk, Oneida, Onondaga,
Cayuga, and Seneca

The Limits of Accommodation

NO LEADER ON LONG Island tried harder to work
within the colonial system than Wyandanch, sachem of the
Montaukett. He did not reflexively resist contact. He
negotiated, aligned, and adapted, believing—as Massasoit
once had—that cooperation might preserve his people's
survival, if not their sovereignty.

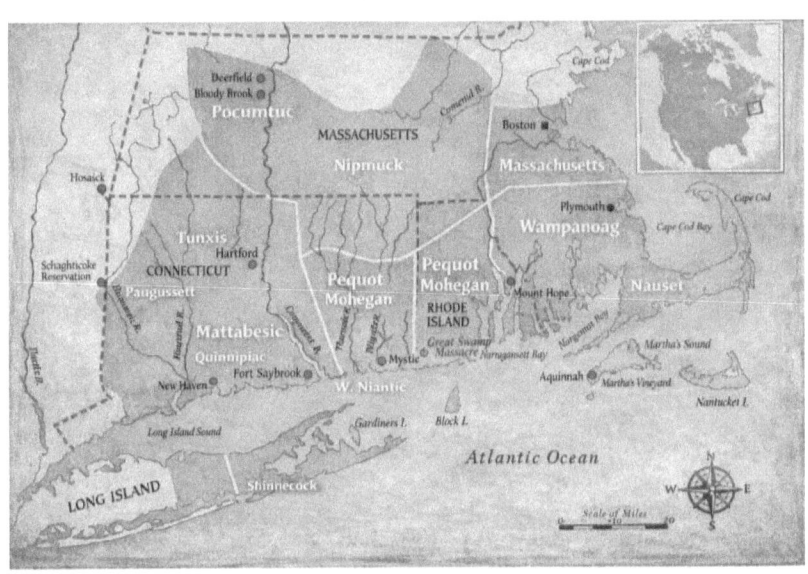

Wyandanch was born in the late 16th or early 17th century on Long Island, in a world still governed by Indigenous rhythms and law. By the time he reached adulthood, that world was already beginning to fracture. His early life coincided with the arrival of English settlements in southern New England, including Plymouth to the north, whose presence would soon reshape the politics of the entire coast. Wyandanch did not come of age in isolation. He grew up hearing reports—first distant, then increasingly close—of what happened to Native nations that misjudged the newcomers.

The lesson that stayed with him arrived in the late 1630s, when news spread of the near-total destruction of the Pequot during the Pequot War. Entire villages had been burned. Survivors were killed, scattered, or sold into slavery. The violence was not confined to warriors. It was absolute. For Wyandanch, the meaning was unmistakable. When it failed, resistance did not lead to negotiation. It led to erasure. From that moment forward, he concluded that survival required a different approach—not defiance, but alignment.

Throughout the mid-seventeenth century, Wyandanch navigated a three-sided struggle that defined Long Island politics. To one side stood Uncas, the ambitious Mohegan sachem whose power was rising through close alliance with the English. To another stood Ninigret, the Niantic leader who pursued his own regional ambitions and openly resisted English influence.

Wyandanch stood between them, governing a people exposed by geography and weakened by disease, with little margin for error. He chose to anchor his position in the English colonies, correctly calculating that colonial support could counterbalance Native rivals even as it narrowed his long-term options.

That calculation was tested in the early 1640s. Miantonomo, the powerful Narragansett leader, unsettled by the accelerating spread of English settlements, sought to organize a pan-Indigenous alliance to strike colonial towns before they became unassailable. In 1640, he approached Wyandanch directly, urging him to join their planned attack on the recently established English coastal villages. Wyandanch refused. He reminded Miantonomo of the Pequot fate, the Mystic River massacre, and the consequences of Indigenous resistance that failed to anticipate English resolve. For the moment, he succeeded in delaying confrontation.

The reprieve did not last. In 1643, the Mohegans went to war and defeated the Narragansetts. Miantonomo was captured by Uncas and executed with colonial approval— another Indigenous leader removed without English hands directly bearing the blood.[1] For Wyandanch, the episode confirmed all he had feared. English power did not need to kill its enemies personally; it only needed to decide who should live and who should not.

Miantonomo's death also reshaped Long Island politics. Before his defeat, Miantonomo had tried to undermine Wyandanch by persuading other Montaukett leaders to sever ties with him and join the Narragansett cause. Wyandanch's refusal to participate, followed by Miantonomo's execution, strengthened his standing within his own community. His authority now rested not on dominance but on foresight—the ability to keep his people alive in a narrowing world.

Plaque displayed at the Wyandanch train station. Shinnecock artist David Bunn Martine created this interpretation of the Sachem's appearance.

Wyandanch's choices were never about victory. They were about endurance. He kept his people tied to the colonists not because he trusted them, but because he understood the fate of those who stood alone. On Long Island, with no

134

interior refuge and no confederacy to retreat into, accommodation was not a moral choice. It was a matter of geography.

English settlements were rapidly expanding across eastern Long Island, and land that Wyandanch believed he was leasing or sharing disappeared into deeds and town charters. Montaukett territory shrank as settlers multiplied. Courts upheld English claims. Wyandanch found himself mediating disputes not between equals but between his people and a legal system designed without them in mind.

In late 1658, Wyandanch entered English legal records in an unexpected way. He lent his canoe—an imposing vessel that may have stretched forty feet—to an English colonist, Jeremy Daily, who intended to use it to transport goods across Long Island Sound. The arrangement was straightforward. Daily would repair the canoe before the voyage and then return it in proper condition. It was a practical exchange, governed by expectation and responsibility rather than a written contract.

Daily failed to uphold his end of the bargain. After reaching Gardiners Island, he neglected the canoe, and when a storm struck, it was badly damaged. Wyandanch responded not with violence or retaliation but with something more revealing. He brought suit against Daily in a colonial court.

The case became one of the earliest recorded trials in which a Native American appeared as a plaintiff against an English defendant in the English colonies. Wyandanch won. The court ordered Daily to pay ten shillings in damages, along with additional court fees.[2] The outcome mattered less for the money than for what it demonstrated: Wyandanch understood English law well enough to use it, and for a moment, that law recognized his claim.

The following year, Wyandanch took another step that reflected both trust and calculation. In 1659, he granted a section of Montaukett land to Lion Gardiner, which would later become the town of Smithtown. At the same time, he gave Gardiner guardianship of his young son, Wyancombone, until the boy could come of age. It was a deeply personal decision—one that tied his family's future to an English ally.

WAYANDANCE, (1) his   mark.

Signature of Wyandanch as he gifts Lion Gardiner a piece of land. Dated July 14. 1659

By the time King Philip's War tore through southern New England, Wyandanch had already chosen his side, and he did so with open eyes. Loyalty to the English was not an abstract gesture or a moral pose; it was a wager made under pressure, shaped by earlier alliances, old debts, and the plain arithmetic of survival. Wyandanch used that loyalty to shield his people wherever he could—to negotiate releases, argue against indiscriminate violence, and position the Montaukett as allies rather than targets. In a war that erased entire villages, that choice mattered. It meant that some Montaukett lived who otherwise would not have.

But loyalty carried a quieter price. Aligning with the English, Wyandanch was pulled away from older Native networks that had once offered a different kind of protection—reciprocal obligation, shared resistance, the moral weight of collective action. After the war, as English victory hardened into dominance, promises thinned. Protection became supervision. Alliance became dependency. The land continued to slip away, acre by acre, deed by deed, until survival itself was redefined as endurance on someone else's terms. What Wyandanch secured was not sovereignty but time, and in the colonial world taking shape around him, time was never neutral.

His death in 1659 was unexpected, and although rumors claimed he was poisoned, no proof was ever found.

What came next was devastating. Wyandanch's wife and son died shortly after him, victims of a plague that spread through Algonquian communities. A daughter, Quashawam, survived and would become influential in her own right, but the leadership structure he had embodied could not be sustained. In the years after his death, the roles of "chief sachem" and "alliance chief" steadily eroded, and once the English completed their conquest of New Netherland, colonial authorities abolished the positions altogether.

Colonial authorities then completed what diplomacy had already undone. The Montaukett were declared extinct as a people under English law, despite the survival of their descendants. Their land passed fully into colonial hands.

Wyandanch had believed that accommodation might preserve a place for his people in a changing world. He used English courts, forged English alliances, and entrusted English guardianship. In the end, none of it outlasted him. What disappeared was not just a leader but a political role—one the English had no intention of allowing to endure.

Wyandanch's story is not one of failure. It is a demonstration of limits. He pursued cooperation with clarity and intent. He understood the risks of resistance and chose the path most likely to preserve his community. What defeated him was not bad faith or miscalculation but the fact that English law did not recognize permanent Indigenous autonomy—even when Indigenous leaders played by its rules.

On Long Island, accommodation delayed dispossession but could not prevent it. The island's leaders learned first what others would learn later: that once settlement became the goal, negotiation could only determine the pace, not the outcome.

[1] John A. Strong, "Wyandanch: Sachem of the Montauks", in Robert Grumet ed., Northeastern Indian Lives, University of Massachusetts Press, 1996
[2] Jacqueline Overton, "Indian life on Long Island: family, work, play, legends, heroes", Volume 23 of Empire State historical publications series, I. J. Friedman, 1963.

Part IV — Mid-Atlantic River Nations (Lenape
Homeland)

Chapter 11 — The Mid-Atlantic World: Rivers of Trade, Corridors of Conquest

The land owns your breath, your dreams, your silence... It is you who belong to her.

—Lenape Elder

LONG BEFORE EUROPEANS CALLED it the Mid-Atlantic, the Lenape knew it as a land of rivers. The Hudson, Delaware, and Susquehanna did not divide the land—they stitched it together. Canoe routes linked tidal estuaries to inland forests; footpaths became arteries of exchange. Shell beads moved north and west. Copper, stone, and furs moved south and east. The Lenape world was one of movement, diplomacy, and negotiation, shaped by seasonal rhythms and long memory.

For countless generations, they planted and harvested the "three sisters," fished in the spring runs of shad and sturgeon, and gathered wild foods from the forests and marshes that stretched from the Hudson's lower reaches to the broad flats of what would later be called the Delaware Bay.

The Lenape world was not a single centralized "nation" so much as a wide homeland (Lenapehoking) made up of many villages and bands that shared related languages, kinship systems, and diplomatic obligations. Within that larger Lenape identity, outsiders and later ethnographers commonly describe three broad regional divisions—Munsee (north), Unami (central), and Unalachtigo (south)—distinguished mainly by where people lived and which dialect they spoke, rather than by rigid political boundaries. In other words: Munsee and Unalachtigo were Lenape, but they sat on different stretches of the same river-and-coast world, and their speech and local alliances reflected that.

The Munsee occupied the northern arc of Lenapehoking, especially around the lower Hudson Valley/New York–New Jersey borderlands and the upper Delaware watershed. Their dialect—Munsee—is the northern branch of the Lenape languages, closely related to Unami but distinct. In practice, Munsee communities were often the Lenape people most immediately entangled with early Dutch and later English pressure around New Netherland/New York and northern New Jersey, making them important borderland diplomats and—when diplomacy failed—frontline survivors in the earliest cycles of displacement.

The Unalachtigo were the southern division of the Lenape, associated with southern New Jersey and the Delaware Bay/coastal plain. Linguistically, they were a Unami-related speech community. In the Lenape world, Unalachtigo communities connected inland river life to the bay and coast through shared trade corridors.

The first Europeans the Lenape encountered were not armies or settlements, but sailors and traders whose ships appeared on the horizon like strange birds.

In 1524, an Italian explorer, Giovanni da Verrazzano, arrived in New York Bay, exchanging cautious greetings with Indigenous people paddling canoes along the coast. When later European groups arrived in the early seventeenth century, they found not a wilderness but a managed landscape. Lenape villages lined the lower Delaware and its tributaries, clustered near fertile floodplains and fishing sites. Cornfields stood where future towns would rise. Fire had long been used to shape forests, attract game, and maintain travel corridors. To European eyes, the land appeared open and inviting. But openness was not absence.

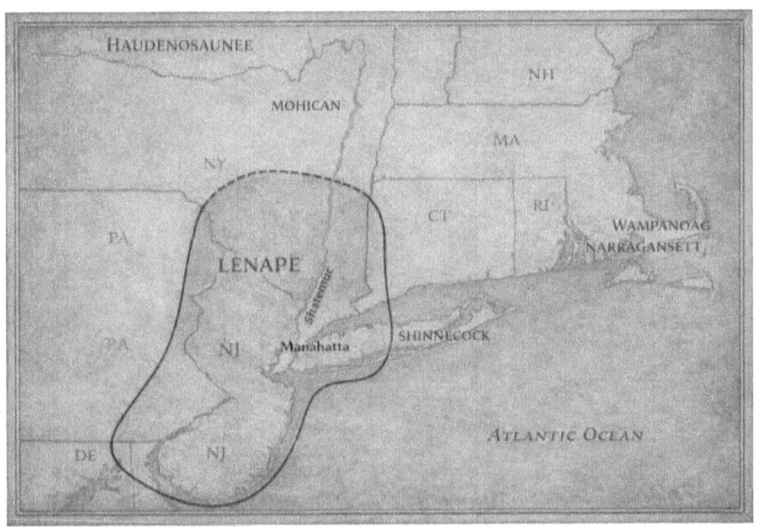

The First Contact

Along the wide mouth of the river, where salt water pushes inland, Lenape fishermen were the first to see it.

At first, it was only a shape, far out on the gray line where sea and sky met. It moved against the wind the way no living thing should. Some thought it was a great fish. They paddled hard for shore and sent runners to the scattered villages and leaders along the coast and upriver: come and see; be ready; something is coming. Soon the shoreline filled—men, women, children—watching as the thing drew nearer, its sides bright with strange colors, its body crowded with life.

As the stories were told, the Lenape did what they always did when the world shifted: they interpreted it through the sacred grammar of their own experience. If something that powerful approached from the sea, it could not be ordinary.

In one of the oldest versions recorded, the leaders and religious specialists debated whether the great being—the Mannitto—was inside it. Preparations began not for war, but for reception: food readied, ceremony considered, the community trying to choose the right posture between fear and reverence. Then came the detail that fixed the conclusion: among the newcomers was a figure dressed in red, glittering with gold lace. To Lenape eyes, he shone with the kind of authority that did not belong to ordinary men. If the visitors were attendants, then the red-coated man must be the one who mattered.[1]

A smaller boat finally slid onto the shore. The red-coated figure stepped forward with companions. They spoke in a language the Lenape did not know. The Lenape answered, as they always had, with formal gestures and watchful courtesy. The first exchange was neither a treaty nor a conquest but a test: who would behave with dignity and who would reveal intent. Then the red-coated man raised a glass. A servant poured a dark liquid—something the

Lenape had never seen—and the visitor drank. He refilled the cup and offered it to the nearest chief.

The cup moved around the circle. One by one, the leaders smelled it and passed it on without tasting. The refusal was not cowardice. It was caution. Accepting a substance from a powerful stranger was not a casual act. In the story as recorded, the moment teetered until a warrior stood. If the visitor drank, he argued, and the gift was offered to them, then refusing it might insult a being with the power to destroy them. Better for one man to risk himself than for an entire people to invite wrath. He took the cup, spoke his farewell, and drank it all.[2]

They watched him like hawks. He staggered. He fell. He slept so deeply that they believed him dead. Then he rose, wonder on his face, and said he had never felt such delight. He asked for more. Soon others drank, then many, until the circle itself dissolved into intoxication. In the story, the strangers withdrew to their vessel while the Lenape were overwhelmed by a drink whose danger they could not yet measure.

Only after this did the newcomers begin to offer what, at first glance, looked like gifts: beads, axes, hoes, stockings. The Lenape accepted them as one accepts powerful objects—carefully, respectfully, sometimes ceremonially. Later, when the visitors returned, they laughed to see axes worn as ornaments and stockings used as pouches. They showed the Lenape how to haft an axe, cut a tree, hoe a field, and wear the cloth. In the story, laughter spread among the Lenape too—not because they were foolish, but because they recognized the strangeness of carrying heavy

147

iron at the throat without knowing its purpose. The world was changing so quickly that even the meaning of a tool could not be assumed.[3]

Then came the request, and with it the hinge of the narrative—the moment the Lenape story treats as the first true revelation of European intent.

The newcomers said they would not stay. They would go away and return. But they needed a little land—just enough to plant a garden and raise herbs and vegetables for their broth. Not a homeland. Not a territory. A small place for fire and food. They asked, in one version, for only as much land as a bullock's hide could cover. The Lenape agreed. It sounded reasonable. The Lenape still had their rivers, forests, and villages; they could afford generosity.

The Europeans took the hide, soaked it, and stretched it outward until it circled a far larger tract than any hide laid flat could have covered. The Lenape were surprised—not because they didn't understand cleverness, but because this cleverness was a weapon. It transformed a social and situational request into an enforceable claim. In some versions, the Lenape chose not to contest it. Why fight over a little ground when there was still so much around them? They would simply be more wary next time.

But the next time came, and then the time after that, and the pattern became clear: each "small" request created a new permanent foothold; each foothold became the basis for another demand. In a version told by Captain Pipe, the 18th-century Lenape diplomat, the newcomers said the first plot was too small to build a fire without being smoked out, so they needed a bit more—this time measured by the woven cords of a chair seat stretched into a boundary, another trick that turned a domestic object into a surveyor's line.

Later tellings sharpened the moral edge. In a retelling by Willie Longbone, the story includes an argument among the Lenape. A man sings of a vision: someone is coming across the water. A warrior says he will kill the newcomer. The visionary insists: no, this one is an elder brother. The disagreement matters because it shows the Lenape story refusing a single emotion—refusing to make first contact with either a purely naive welcome or pure suspicion. It was debated, contested, and weighed.

Taken together, the versions are not merely stories about a ship. They are a Lenape explanation of how an encounter became dispossession: awe becoming familiarity, familiarity dependence, dependence loss—each step plausible in isolation, devastating in accumulation. The "bullock hide" is the symbol because it turns relationships into measurements and measurements into ownership. It marks the moment the Lenape story identifies as the beginning of a world where words can be trapped on paper and then used against the people who spoke them.

Trade Grows Along the Delaware

By 1609, Dutch ships were routinely probing the Hudson River, and within a decade, traders were moving inland, exchanging metal goods, cloth, and weapons for beaver pelts. They arrived like tidewater: advancing, retreating, advancing again, until what had seemed temporary became irreversible. Now the Lenape engaged readily. Trade was familiar; alliances could be managed. The beaver trade pulled Lenape communities deeper into Atlantic markets and drew the attention of powerful neighbors to the north and west.

Illustration, Dutch ship in the Hudson River

Disease arrived even faster than settlers. Long before English towns took root along the Delaware, Lenape communities were already absorbing blows from epidemics carried inland by traders, sailors, and displaced peoples. Between roughly 1616 and the 1650s, successive waves of smallpox, measles, and influenza swept through the Mid-Atlantic river valleys and coastal plains. Contemporary observers and later historians estimate that as much as one-third to one-half of the Lenape population may have died during this period, with some local communities suffering even higher losses.[4] The devastation was uneven but relentless, arriving in intervals that prevented recovery before the next outbreak struck.

The damage went far beyond numbers. Epidemic disease severed kinship chains and destabilized leadership structures that depended on continuity and consensus. Elders died before passing on ceremonial knowledge, and heirs were lost before assuming responsibility. Villages that had anchored seasonal cycles of planting, hunting, and diplomacy were abandoned or merged with neighboring villages.

Councils still met, and treaties were still debated, but under strain, with fewer voices and diminished leverage. Power shifted internally and regionally, reshaping alliances at the very moment Europeans began formalizing their presence.

This mattered profoundly when sustained colonization followed. The Lenape did not meet the English from a position of full strength or outright defeat. They stood instead in a weakened middle ground—still numerous and organized, yet bearing losses that outsiders often mistook for decline or absence. English settlers interpreted cleared fields and empty villages as signs of divine favor or unused land. The Lenape saw them as scars.

By the time figures like Tamanend emerged as diplomatic leaders, they were negotiating not only with newcomers but also with the lingering consequences of catastrophe—seeking to preserve autonomy in a world already altered by forces beyond human intent.

As Europeans began building permanent towns along the Delaware in the 1620s and 1630s, the balance had permanently shifted. Dutch, Swedish, and later English settlers competed for access to land and river corridors, each empire layering its claims atop the last. The Lenape, positioned at the crossroads of these ambitions, sought accommodation. Land agreements were made—understood by Lenape leaders as shared use, seasonal access, or symbolic alliance. Europeans recorded them as absolute and permanent.

As settlements multiplied, space collapsed. What had once been negotiable boundaries became surveyed lines. Rivers once shared became controlled. The Lenape were pressed from all sides: Europeans advancing from the coast, the Haudenosaunee pressing from the north during the Beaver Wars, and rival colonial governments treating Lenape neutrality as a weakness.

The Lenape story is not one of immediate conquest. In the early decades of European contact, the Lenape remained powerful and numerous. They outnumbered the few hundred traders and settlers who first arrived at their rivers and creeks. They controlled access to interior corridors and set the terms of most early exchanges. For decades, Lenape leaders maneuvered carefully, using diplomacy, trade, and strategic restraint to delay the inevitable. They played colonial powers against one another, relocated villages, absorbed refugees, and renegotiated alliances. Survival, not resistance, defined the era.

But within a few decades, those terms would be transformed by disease, trade dependency, and colonial expansion—forces that moved faster than any canoe and reshaped the Lenape world before many communities fully understood what was happening.

The chiefs we encounter next did not inherit a stable world. They led amid collapse and compression, forced to make decisions with diminishing options. Their authority rested not on domination, but on persuasion—on holding together communities under pressure few societies could withstand.

This was the Mid-Atlantic at the moment of reckoning: not yet conquered, but no longer secure; still Indigenous, but rapidly becoming colonial. The Lenape stood at the center of it all—river people in a world where rivers had become highways of empire.

[1] James Rementer, The Arrival of the Europeans as Told by the Lenape (Delaware Tribe of Indians).

[2] Rementer, Arrival of the Europeans.

[3] Rementer, Arrival of the Europeans.

[4] Jean R. Soderlund, "Native Peoples to 1680," Encyclopedia of Greater Philadelphia

Tamanend

Chief of Chiefs and Chief of the Turtle Clan(Pùkuwànku),

Lenape Nation

1625 – c. 1701

Chapter 12 – Tamanend, Lenape

...that there be goodwill and tranquility between the indigenous people of this land and those who occupy it now, as long as the rivers and creeks flow, and the sun, moon, and stars shine.

—Chief Tamanend, Lenape

BY THE TIME EUROPEANS began writing Tamanend's name into their records, the Lenape world was already narrowing. Rivers that had once carried trade now carried settlers. Footpaths hardened into roads. Agreements multiplied even as the ground beneath them shifted. Tamanend did not inherit a moment of first contact, nor the raw shock of epidemic collapse. He inherited something more dangerous: the illusion of stability.

Tamanend emerged as a leader in the late seventeenth century, when the Lenape were still numerous, still present, and indispensable to colonial survival—but no longer secure. He was a sachem known less for warfare than for judgment, a man whose authority rested on restraint and reputation rather than force.

Among his people, he was respected as a speaker and mediator. Among Europeans, particularly the English of Pennsylvania, he came to be regarded as a model of reasonableness. That reputation would follow him long after his death, reshaped to suit colonial memory.

Born around 1625, Tamanend was the Lenape Nation's Chief of Chiefs and the Chief of the Turtle (Pùkuwànku) in the Delaware Valley. He lived through a revolving door of European regimes—first the Swedes, then the Dutch, and finally the English, who seized New Netherland in 1664 and began treating the river corridor as an extension of their Atlantic empire.

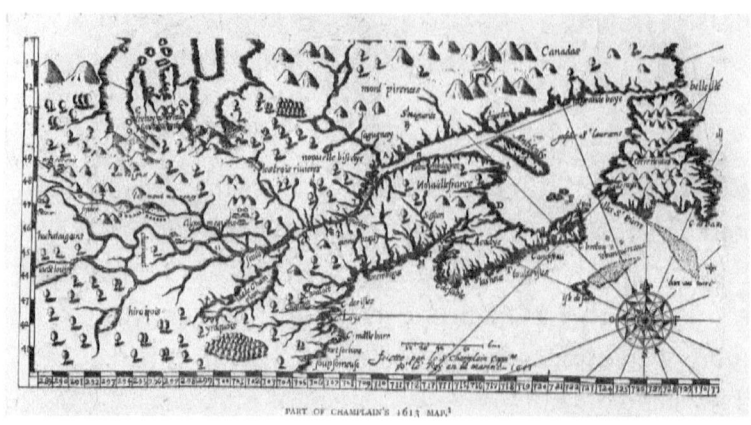

PART OF CHAMPLAIN'S 1613 MAP.

Flags changed, but the pressure on Lenape life remained constant: more ships, more traders, more demands, more paper. The newcomers came first for furs and provisions, then for timber and farmland. With every season, the river carried not only goods but also rumors of new settlements upriver, new claims, and new boundaries that existed nowhere on the land.

Tamanend spent these decades doing the unglamorous work that kept a people intact. He managed trade relationships and the disputes that inevitably followed. He negotiated access to planting grounds and fisheries as strangers began fencing off what had always been shared. He mediated quarrels sparked by alcohol, theft, and retaliation—small incidents that could ignite larger conflicts if left unattended.

Above all, he watched how Europeans recorded agreements: how a conversation became a "deed," how temporary permission hardened into a permanent claim, and how words spoken in reciprocity could be captured on paper and later wielded as a weapon.

By the time William Penn stepped onto the Delaware shore, Tamanend's greatest asset was not idealism—it was experience. He had seen Europeans come and go, promises made and revised, and the gap between a courteous meeting and the slow grind of settlement that followed. If he chose diplomacy with Penn, it was not because he believed the Lenape had nothing to fear. It was because he understood exactly what they had—and did not—have to gain by refusing.

Under the Elm Tree

When William Penn arrived in the Delaware Valley in the early 1680s, he brought a vision of peaceful settlement unlike anything the region had yet seen—or so he claimed. He spoke of fair dealing, religious tolerance, and a negotiated coexistence.

Tamanend's role in accepting that vision began beneath an elm tree.

Sometime in the early 1680s, at Shakamaxon, a gathering place along the Delaware River, Lenape leaders met with Penn and representatives of the newly established Pennsylvania colony. No fort guarded the meeting, and no troops stood nearby. The setting itself was the message: open ground, shared space, a deliberate contrast to the violence that had already scarred New England and Virginia.

Tamanend listened. Unlike many earlier encounters, this was not a meeting between desperate settlers and dominant Indigenous powers, nor between conquerors and the defeated. It was a negotiation on a fragile middle ground, where both sides believed that restraint might still preserve the future.

For Penn, the meeting embodied his vision of a colony founded without bloodshed. For Tamanend, it was a negotiation shaped by long experience—an effort to preserve Lenape autonomy amid a world already shifting beneath his feet.

Illustration of Tamanend and William Penn, Public Domain

The agreement traditionally associated with Penn and Tamanend, later romanticized as the "Great Treaty," was never written down. That absence matters. Furthermore, it was not a single treaty but a series of understandings, renewed and reaffirmed over time. Between 1683 and the end of the decade, Penn and Tamanend signed or confirmed at least seven agreements, each reiterating commitments to peace, mutual aid, and restraint.[1]

These were not land cessions in the rigid European sense but assurances of coexistence—promises that settlers would live among the Lenape rather than replace them.

To Lenape leaders, such agreements were living arrangements sustained by continued good conduct and mutual respect. Their power lay not in parchment but in relationship. To Penn and his successors, they were proof that land could be acquired without violence and sanctified by consent rather than conquest. Each side believed it had secured peace, but each meant something different by it.

It was in this context that Tamanend is remembered for saying that the Lenape and the English would "live in peace as long as the waters run in the rivers and creeks and as long as the stars and moon endure." These words endure because they express the Lenape understanding of permanence: peace measured against the natural world, not human institutions.

Later generations carved the phrase into stone and bronze, fixing it in civic memory. Yet the deeper meaning lies in what followed. The rivers kept flowing. The stars and moon endured. The peace did not.

Sculpture of Tamanend

For a time, the arrangement held. Pennsylvania expanded without the immediate bloodshed that marked New England or Virginia. Tamanend's diplomacy brought decades of relative calm, allowing Lenape communities to remain in their homelands longer than many of their neighbors. But peace did not stop settlement; it merely slowed its consequences. Survey lines crept outward. Courts replaced councils. What had been shared space became private property.

The public memory freezes him beneath the elm at Shakamaxon, but the real work came after the handshakes: repeated meetings, renewed understandings, and ongoing problem-solving as more ships arrived and more fences went up. The Quaker policy of peace mattered, but it did not remove the underlying pressure. It simply changed how that pressure was applied—through negotiations, paperwork, and "purchases" that multiplied as the colony grew.

Tamanend died sometime around 1701. His legacy of leadership passed to several of his grandchildren, who became important Lenape chiefs and warriors, including Pisquetomen, Nenatcheehunt, Shingas, and Tamaqua.

By the early eighteenth century, the limits of accommodation were clear. The Lenape found themselves increasingly constrained, and their political authority undermined by new colonial officials who favored compliant leaders and written deeds. Tamanend's legacy— measured, principled, and ultimately overwhelmed—came to symbolize both the possibility and the failure of coexistence in the American founding era. His promise to the English was not naïve; it was conditional. What failed was not the Lenape vision of coexistence but the colonial willingness to honor it beyond the moment of need.

In later generations, Americans would elevate Tamanend to the status of a legend, celebrating him as a symbol of harmony while ignoring the dispossession that followed. Towns, societies, and even political clubs would bear his name. The man himself, however, had sought something simpler and far more difficult: a way for his people to remain where they had always lived, in a world that was rapidly deciding they could not.

[1] Benjamin Franklin, Pennsylvania, and the First Nations: The Treaties of 1736-62. Ukraine: University of Illinois Press, 2006.

Teedyuscung
"King of the Delawares" Lenape
1700–1763

Chapter 13 — Teedyuscung: Voice in the Ruins

The earth is life, and the land is our home.

— Hadrien Coumans

THE ROAD THAT CARRIED Teedyuscung into Easton, Pennsylvania, in the summer of 1757 was already heavy with blood. It cut through a landscape broken by two decades of false treaties, burned cabins, abandoned farms, and towns that no longer trusted the names they used to give themselves. The war between Britain and France had turned Pennsylvania's frontier into a killing ground, but the violence did not begin there. It began years earlier, in rooms filled with paper and ink, where promises were stretched until they tore.

Teedyuscung had learned early that the Lenape were expected to disappear politely.

But it had not always been that way. A generation earlier, the Lenape, had been the acknowledged people of the Delaware River valley. Their towns lined the water; their fields fed both Native and European mouths. But by the 1730s, they were repeatedly and publicly told that they were no longer a nation capable of speaking for itself. They were dismissed as "women," a political insult implying weakness and dependency, placed under the authority of the Iroquois Confederacy by colonial officials who found the arrangement convenient.

The Lenape were not consulted. They were informed. This was Teedyuscung's narrowing world. He had known Christianity, alcohol, and poverty. He had wandered, preached, failed, and returned. His early life was marked less by distinction than by collapse. Yet the dispossession of his people gave him a purpose that steadied him. If the English insisted on denying Lenape sovereignty, he would force them to hear a Lenape voice.

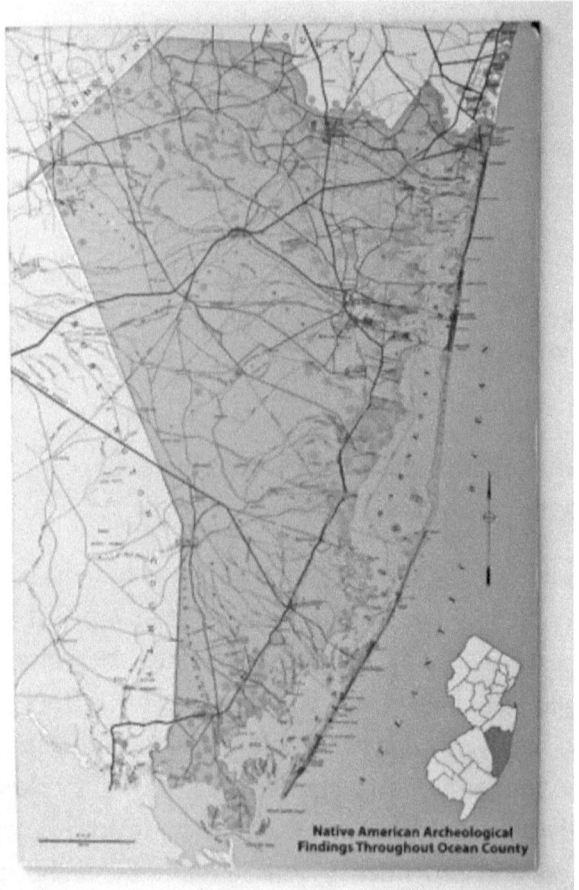

Native American Archeological Findings Throughout Ocean County

Dispossession

Teedyuscung—whose name loosely translates as "as far as the wood's edge"—was born around 1700 near what is now Trenton, New Jersey, at a moment when the Lenape world was already receding. By the time he reached adulthood, many of the Lenape along the lower Delaware had been drawn deep into the orbit of colonial life. They wore European clothes, traded for European goods, worshipped in Christian churches, and spoke English alongside their own language. Teedyuscung grew up fluent in both worlds, though fully secure in neither.

Alcohol, introduced freely by traders, would haunt him for much of his life. It weakened families, eroded authority, and followed him long after his people were forced from their land. By 1730, pressure from settlers had driven the Lenape out of the Trenton area altogether. Teedyuscung moved west with his wife and son, settling near the confluence of the Delaware and Lehigh Rivers in present-day eastern Pennsylvania. Even there, the refuge proved temporary.

After this move, Teedyuscung encountered Lenape communities less altered by colonial influence—people who still practiced ancestral ceremonies and held fast to older forms of leadership and belief. The contrast sharpened his awareness of what had been lost. As colonial Pennsylvania expanded, the Lenape were forced into negotiations they had not chosen, and Teedyuscung emerged as a spokesman for a people increasingly discussed but rarely heard.

Walking Purchase, 1737

The decisive blow came in 1737 with the Walking Purchase, a land fraud that stripped the Lenape of much of the Lehigh Valley.[1] The loss confirmed what many already feared: that agreements with the colony were weapons disguised as words. As his biographer later observed, Teedyuscung was torn in his response to white society. He was drawn to European authority by insecurity and the collapse of traditional Lenape power, yet that same sense of humiliation fueled a fierce rejection of colonial control. He admired what he resisted and resisted what he admired—a tension that would define his leadership.[2]

King of the Delawares

In 1754, Teedyuscung left the Moravian settlement and moved north into the Wyoming Valley, where displaced Native communities had gathered along the Susquehanna. By this time, the frontier was in flames. The French and

Indian War had pushed violence eastward, and Lenape warriors—driven from their lands and promised restitution by French agents—had joined attacks on Pennsylvania settlements. Farmhouses burned. Families fled. The Quaker colony that had once prided itself on peace now begged London for troops.

Settlers did not stop when the Lenape moved west. They followed.

By the early 1750s, the Wyoming Valley had become a corridor of encroachment, and the Lenape who had taken refuge there found themselves pressed from every direction. From the east, settlers from Connecticut claimed the Wyoming Valley and much of northern Pennsylvania under distant charters that ignored the people already living on the land. From the west came the French and their Native allies, determined to halt British expansion beyond the Alleghenies. From the south came Pennsylvanians armed with grants issued in Philadelphia, paper titles that carried more weight than centuries of occupation.

The pressure was not only political. A severe drought struck the region, cutting harvests and sharpening hunger. The Lenape were running out of space, time, and food.

Teedyuscung first turned to Pennsylvania's colonial government for protection or relief. He was redirected to the Iroquois Six Nations, whose authority over the Lenape existed largely in the colonial imagination yet was convenient to invoke. The result was paralysis. Neither the Six Nations nor Governor Robert Morris offered meaningful aid. When French-allied Native warriors attacked the Wyoming Valley, the Lenape were left exposed.

Faced with abandonment, Teedyuscung made a choice shaped more by survival than by ideology. He aligned his warriors with the western Delaware and, by extension, with the French. The alliance did not end the violence; it formalized it.

Raids followed. Teedyuscung and other Lenape leaders attacked colonial settlements across eastern Pennsylvania, acts of retaliation for decades of land seizures disguised as legal transactions. The so-called previous land purchases had stripped the Lenape of their homeland without firing a shot. Now the conflict returned in kind.

Yet even as the frontier exploded into chaos, Teedyuscung did not abandon diplomacy. He traveled east to meet colonial officials in Philadelphia and Easton, determined to force the colony to confront what it had done.

Easton, 1758

It was in Easton that he stepped onto the colonial stage as a central figure in negotiations between Pennsylvania's Native peoples and the government in Philadelphia, determined—at last—to speak for himself and for those silenced.

He spoke plainly. He did not flatter. He accused. It was a bluntness that startled his listeners. The root of the war, he said, was theft. The Walking Purchase of 1737—a fraud in which colonial officials claimed far more land than had ever been agreed—had stripped the Lenape of their homeland. They had been pushed west, then again, until there was nowhere left to go.

The violence, Teedyuscung insisted, was not savagery but a consequence. His words unsettled the room. Colonial negotiators were accustomed to deference and to speeches that could be translated into harmless ritual. Teedyuscung offered neither. He spoke as if the English were accountable. Worse, he spoke as if the Lenape still mattered.

Striking the ground beneath his feet, he delivered an accusation that could not be translated away:

This very ground that is under me was my land and inheritance, and is taken from me by fraud.

It was not a metaphor. It was a statement of record.

It was there that he declared himself "King of the Delawares." The title was less a claim of dominance than a declaration of survival. Pennsylvania's leaders also needed a scapegoat and a solution. Teedyuscung offered both, though not in the way they expected.

For a moment, it worked. Pennsylvania officials, desperate to stabilize the frontier, agreed, at least in principle, to recognize Lenape grievances. They promised to investigate the Walking Purchase, to provide land security, and to ensure peace. Teedyuscung believed, or chose to believe, that this time was different.

He returned west as a man marked by possibility. Moravian missionaries, who saw in him both spiritual promise and political utility, helped establish a new Lenape town at

Wyoming along the Susquehanna River. There, Teedyuscung attempted something rare in colonial America: a community grounded in diplomacy rather than war, where Lenape autonomy might survive the tightening grip of empire.

Teedyuscung, Illustration

Wyoming became a symbol—and a target.

Teedyuscung's authority rested on a fragile balance. Many Lenape warriors distrusted him, seeing diplomacy as a weakness. Others resented his reliance on missionaries and his willingness to speak in English political terms. Meanwhile, colonial officials continued to undercut him by negotiating separately with the Iroquois. The contradictions pressed in from every side.

When the war shifted again, and British victories made Native alliances less valuable, Teedyuscung's usefulness faded. Promises made at Easton were delayed, diluted, and quietly forgotten. Investigations went nowhere. Land was not returned. The frontier violence continued, now justified as defense.

Teedyuscung protested. He traveled. He spoke. Each journey weakened his standing at home, while each unkept promise strengthened his enemies. By 1763, the year of Pontiac's uprising, the Susquehanna Valley was no longer safe. Settlers poured in. Militia bands roamed freely. In Pennsylvania, anger turned inward. The Paxton Boys—frontiersmen convinced that all Native people were enemies—murdered the peaceful Conestoga Indians and marched on Philadelphia, demanding more blood.

Wyoming, 1763

Teedyuscung condemned them. His words carried little weight. In April 1763, his town at Wyoming was burned.

The fire came at night. Whether set by hostile Native rivals, colonial agents, or settlers acting on rumor has never been proven. What is known is that Teedyuscung died in the flames, trapped in his own house. The leader who had tried to anchor peace perished as war closed in on him. His death passed quickly through colonial newspapers. There was no investigation. No reckoning. Another Indian leader had vanished, as expected.

Yet Teedyuscung's significance lies not in his failure but in what he exposed. He showed that Native resistance did not always take the form of war cries and raids. It could instead appear in council chambers, spoken in measured sentences and grounded in documents the colonists themselves had written. He forced Pennsylvania to confront its own paper trail—and, in doing so, revealed how deeply colonial expansion depended on legal fictions as much as on force.

Teedyuscung also revealed the cost of negotiating with an empire that had no intention of stopping. He was destroyed not for being ineffective but for being briefly effective—making dispossession visible.

After his death, the Lenape were pushed farther west. The treaties multiplied. The maps filled in. The space for voices like his narrowed to silence. But for a moment, standing before governors and agents, Teedyuscung spoke as if the future were still undecided. He spoke as if words could hold land in place. He was wrong—but the attempt itself mattered. In the long history of America's frontier, Teedyuscung stands as a reminder that collapse is not always the absence of leadership. Sometimes it is the deliberate destruction of it.

[1] Wallace, Anthony F.C. (1949). King of the Delawares: Teedyuscung (1700–1763). Philadelphia: University of Pennsylvania Press.
[2] Wallace, King of the Delawares.

Part V — Chesapeake and the Powhatan World

Chapter 14 — The Chesapeake Waterways

When the blood in your veins returns to the sea, and the earth in your bones returns to the ground, perhaps then you will remember that this land does not belong to you, it is you who belongs to this land.

— Native American Proverb

THE CHESAPEAKE WAS NOT a place that revealed itself quickly. Its coastline dissolved into water, its rivers ran inland for hundreds of miles, and its forests pressed so close to the shore that land and sea seemed to merge. To arrive by ship was to enter a world without clear edges—an estuary so vast it behaved like an inland sea, fed by tidal rivers that carried salt water deep into the continent. The land was low, fertile, and teeming with life. It invited settlement, but it also concealed power.

For millennia, this was a populated and organized world. Algonquian-speaking peoples occupied the tidewater region in dense networks of towns and villages, bound by kinship, tribute, and seasonal movement. They farmed corn, beans, and squash in cleared fields along the rivers, fished the estuary with weirs and nets, hunted deer and other game in the surrounding forests, and traveled primarily by water. Canoes were roads here. Rivers were not barriers but arteries, linking communities from the coast to the fall line.

The Chesapeake was never just a bay. It was a living system. Along its western shore rose the domain later labeled the Powhatan Confederacy, a loose yet formidable network of Algonquian-speaking peoples bound by tribute, kinship, and calculated force. The Powhatan, Pamunkey, Chickahominy, Mattaponi, Rappahannock, Nansemond, Appomattoc, Arrohateck, Kiskiack, and Paspahegh were not satellites orbiting a single capital so much as communities woven into a system that rewarded cooperation and punished defiance. Authority flowed outward from the paramount chief, but it was enforced locally, village by village, river by river, in a landscape where cornfields and fishing weirs mattered as much as warriors.

At the edges of that system lived people whose position made them both valuable and vulnerable. The Chesapeake (Chesepian), settled near the mouth of the bay, occupied ground exposed to the open Atlantic and to the earliest European ships. The Patawomeck along the Potomac controlled a northern gateway—one foot in the Chesapeake world, the other pointed toward the interior. These border people understood before most that geography could be destiny. To sit astride a river mouth or a major tributary was to invite trade, intrusion, and eventual pressure to choose sides in conflicts not of their making.

North of the Potomac, the Chesapeake continues into what would become Maryland, where river nations like the Piscataway, Patuxent, Conoy, Nanticoke, Choptank, and

Annamessex shaped a parallel world of estuaries and marshlands. These communities were defined by water: by seasonal movement between fishing camps and planting grounds, by shell middens that marked generations of return, by rivers that connected them to the bay and to one another. When Europeans arrived, these waterways became channels not just for trade but for jurisdictional confusion—competing colonial claims layered atop Native landscapes that had never recognized straight lines or surveyed borders.

Across the bay on the Virginia Eastern Shore, the Accomac (Accohannock), Gingaskin, Assateague, and Wicocomico lived closer to the sea than to the inland capitals of power. Their orientation was outward, toward fishing grounds, barrier islands, and seasonal abundance. Distance offered initial insulation, but it also meant isolation as English expansion accelerated. The shore would become a place where accommodation often replaced resistance—not because the people lacked resolve, but because the math of survival favored delay over confrontation.

Beyond the tidewater, the Piedmont and interior connector peoples—the Monacan, Manahoac, Nottoway, Occaneechi, Saponi, Tutelo (Nahyssan), and Meherrin—occupied the hinge between worlds. They controlled overland routes linking the Chesapeake to the mountains and the Carolina interior, making them essential intermediaries long before Europeans understood the terrain. These nations felt the pull of coastal politics without sharing in its immediate rewards, and they absorbed pressure from multiple directions as English settlement pushed west and rival Native powers maneuvered for advantage.

They serve as a reminder that what happened on the water never stays there. The bay was the stage, but the consequences radiated inland, following rivers upstream and trails into the woods, reshaping the entire region long before the outlines of colonies were fully drawn.

When Europeans arrived in the Chesapeake in the early seventeenth century, the land seemed open. The rivers welcomed ships far inland. Villages appeared scattered and unfortified. To English eyes trained in European warfare, the scene looked empty. It was not. It was a landscape shaped by generations of deliberate use—burned, planted, harvested, and defended according to rhythms outsiders could not see.

To the people who lived there, this was not a margin but a resource: fisheries, oyster beds, and tidal flats that fed towns clustered just inland. The coast was open, but it was not undefended. Movement along it was watched, negotiated, and remembered.

Inland, authority followed the tide.

The Powhatan Confederacy wielded power and authority. Leadership rested on control of food, access to trade goods, and the ability to manage conflict. Power was personal, negotiated, and always vulnerable. Their reach extended only as far upriver as salt water could travel. The tidal reaches of the James, York, Rappahannock, and Potomac rivers marked the practical limits of political control. Canoes could transport tribute, food, and messengers through the estuary and along the rivers, binding distant communities into a shared system. Fields could be planted in fertile floodplains. Fish runs could be predicted and exploited. Control of the water meant control of communication, sustenance, and diplomacy.

Below the fall line, where tides rose and fell, and boats could move easily, the confederacy held sway. Above it, where rivers narrowed, shallowed, and broke into rapids, Powhatan influence weakened and gave way to other peoples with different alliances and priorities.

The fall line—where the tide finally gave way to stone—was both a geographic and a political threshold. It marked the edge of the Chesapeake lowlands and the beginning of a different world: upland forests, smaller streams, and independent groups less tied to the estuary. Powhatan leaders did not seek to rule beyond this point. Their power was strongest where the land remained wet, open, and navigable.

To the English, these watery boundaries were easy to misread. Rivers looked like highways into the interior, not the edges of a political order. Ships pushed upstream past villages that regarded those waters as theirs. The colonists saw access. The Powhatan saw intrusion.

The geography of the Chesapeake shaped the confederacy's strength—and its vulnerability. The same open waterways that enabled Powhatan authority to extend across hundreds of miles also allowed English ships to penetrate deep into the region's heart. Control of the tide had once unified the Powhatan world. In time, it would expose it.

The Virginia Company, 1607

European contact in the Chesapeake began in earnest in the spring of 1607, when three English ships entered the bay's mouth and turned south into a broad river the newcomers would name the James. They came from England under the authority of the Virginia Company of London, carrying instructions to secure profit, passage, and permanence. Their chosen settlement site was Jamestown, a marshy peninsula deep within Powhatan territory, selected less by wisdom than for defensibility against European rivals. From the moment they anchored, the English were visible, vulnerable, and dependent.

English ships circa 1607

Native leaders responded with caution shaped by experience. Europeans were not unknown quantities; earlier Spanish expeditions had passed along the coast, bringing violence and disease. The English were approached as potential assets rather than immediate enemies—foreigners who might be absorbed into existing political systems as trading partners or clients. Food was exchanged. Messages were carried. Boundaries were tested. The English believed this restraint was submission, failing to recognize they were being assessed rather than welcomed.

The first winter, the newcomers survived only because they were fed. Their numbers were small, their health poor, and their plans unworkable. They relied on Native corn, hunters, guides, and patience. In return, they offered copper, metal tools, cloth, and glass beads—items that circulated quickly through Chesapeake trade networks, altering status relationships and expectations. What began as an exchange carried hidden costs. European goods unsettled established authority, and European diseases— moving invisibly and relentlessly—began thinning Native populations well beyond the reach of English settlements.

The catastrophe unfolded slowly, then all at once. The English did not leave. Jamestown hardened into a foothold, then a claim. Fields spread. Fences appeared. Rivers became lines of possession. What had been cautious coexistence became competition for land, and that competition hardened into conflict. Indigenous leaders who had once sought to manage the newcomers found themselves confronting a people who measured belonging not by relationship but by ownership. The Chesapeake had absorbed strangers before. This time, the strangers intended to stay.

Smallpox and other epidemics spread faster than treaties or guns, hollowing out communities and destabilizing power. Political balances shifted, and old rivalries resurfaced.

Tribute systems frayed under pressure. As English settlements hardened into towns and plantations, the Chesapeake's rivers became borders rather than highways, dividing Native land into parcels measured on paper.

Conflict was not immediate, but it was inevitable. The geography that had sustained Native power—open waterways, fertile soil, easy movement—also made the region irresistible to colonists who did not intend to leave. What began as contact became competition. What began as coexistence hardened into conquest.

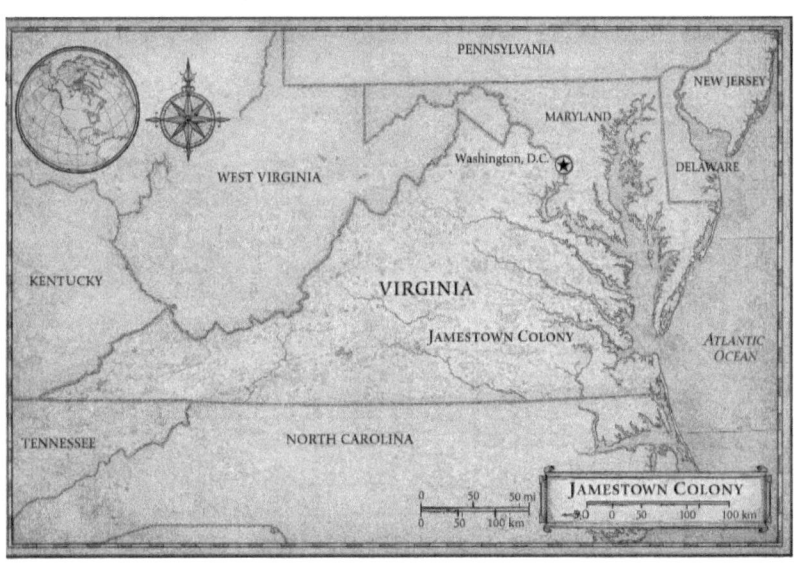

Map, Illustration, Jamestown Colony

This was the world into which the great Chesapeake leaders emerged: men and women navigating a collapsing order, trying to bend a flood rather than stop it outright. Their stories unfold against water and forest, diplomacy and betrayal, survival and loss—shaped as much by the land itself as by the people who fought to remain on it.

Powhatan (Wahunsenacawh)

Chief, Powhatan Confederacy

1547 – c. 1618

Chapter 15 — Powhatan, Powhatan Confederacy

Why will you take by force what you may have quietly by love? Why will you destroy us who supply you with food? What can you get by war?

— Powhatan

THE ENGLISH ARRIVED IN Powhatan's world by water, and it was water that first betrayed them. Their ships slid into the Chesapeake in the spring of 1607, following a maze of channels that widened and narrowed with the tide, carrying salt far inland. Every bend of river lay within a web of occupation and surveillance that the English did not yet understand.

Master of the Tide

Powhatan was not a king in the European sense, though the English insisted on calling him one. He was a paramount chief, the central figure in a confederacy of Algonquian-speaking peoples whose towns lined the tidal rivers of what is now coastal Virginia. His authority extended as far as canoes could travel with the tide and no farther. Beyond the fall line—where rivers turned shallow and rocky—his influence faded into other worlds.

By the time the English arrived, Powhatan had spent decades consolidating power. Through marriage alliances, calculated violence, and selective generosity, he had drawn dozens of communities into his orbit. Tribute came in the form of corn, skins, and labor. In return, he offered protection, mediation, and access to trade. It was a river-based empire, held together not by walls or armies but by the Chesapeake landscape—fertile floodplains, predictable fish runs, and rivers that served as highways rather than borders.

When the English founded Jamestown, they did so deep within this system, though they did not recognize it as such. They arrived with fragile numbers, little food, and extravagant expectations. Within weeks, they were dependent on Native corn. Within months, they were dependent on Powhatan's restraint.

Powhatan (Wahunsenacaw)

Powhatan was not his birth name. He was born around 1571 and named Wahunsenacaw. When the colonists arrived in 1607, they came to know him as Powhatan, a title derived from one of his principal towns near the falls of the James River, close to present-day Richmond. The English assumed it was a personal name. In truth, it was a place—and a seat of power.

By then, Powhatan had already achieved what few leaders in the region had. Through alliance, coercion, and careful diplomacy, he had assembled a confederacy of roughly thirty Algonquian-speaking communities, binding an estimated ten to fifteen thousand people into a single political system.

Powhatan approached the newcomers with measured caution. Europeans were not unfamiliar—Spanish ships had passed along the coast before—but permanent settlement was new. He assessed the English as potential assets: troublesome, poorly organized, yet possibly useful as trading partners or subordinate allies. Food was provided sparingly. Contact was tightly controlled. Messages were exchanged through intermediaries. The English mistook this measured engagement for friendship.

The misunderstanding cut both ways. The English believed themselves destined to command the land. Powhatan believed the English could be absorbed into his political world, made dependent and therefore manageable. Each side assumed time favored them.

But only one side would benefit.

Collapse, War, and an Uneasy Peace

Jamestown nearly failed before it truly began. By the winter of 1609–1610, the settlement had reached the brink of extinction during what colonists later called the Starving Time. Leadership had fractured, supplies were gone, and relations with surrounding Native communities had collapsed into hostility. The English had overreached— demanding food, trespassing on fields, and mistaking Powhatan's restraint for weakness. In response, Powhatan tightened the noose. Villages cut off trade. Hunting parties were driven away. English foraging became a death sentence.

Powhatan did not need to storm Jamestown to defeat it. He knew the colony survived only because of Native tolerance. When that tolerance ended, the settlement withered. By the spring of 1610, the English abandoned Jamestown altogether, loading survivors onto boats and drifting

downriver toward the Chesapeake, prepared to leave
Virginia behind. Only the chance arrival of a relief fleet
forced them back. Jamestown survived, but barely—and
only because Powhatan had not finished the work.

Illustration, Jamestown

Meanwhile, English demands grew. They wanted more
food, more land, and more permanence. What had begun as
a tentative accommodation hardened into a contest of wills.

Conflict flared, receded, and returned. Raids were met with
reprisals. Hostages were taken and exchanged. At times,
Powhatan restrained violence, calculating that the English
presence could still be managed. At other moments, he

sanctioned force, testing whether they could be driven out. The geography that had once strengthened his position— the openness of the rivers—now allowed English ships to push ever farther inland.

Disease struck. Epidemics—likely smallpox and other Old-World illnesses—rippled through the Chesapeake, weakening communities and eroding the very networks that sustained Powhatan's authority. The English, though fewer in number, were replenished by ships. Powhatan's losses could not be so easily replaced.

The English also misunderstood Powhatan himself. They fixated on him, believing that removing or converting him would collapse the confederacy. In truth, his power was already under strain. Tributary groups questioned the value of allegiance, and younger leaders eyed autonomy. The political order Powhatan had built was resilient, but not immune to sustained pressure from settlements that did not retreat.

What followed was open war. The First Anglo-Powhatan War, beginning in 1609, hardened relations that had once been flexible. English forces adopted scorched-earth tactics, burning villages and destroying crops. Powhatan warriors responded with ambushes and attrition. Neither side achieved a decisive victory. Instead, the conflict settled into exhaustion. Powhatan could not expel the English entirely; the English could not subdue the Chesapeake interior without Native food and knowledge. The land itself resisted conquest.

The turning point came not on the battlefield but through capture. In 1613, Captain Samuel Argall seized Pocahontas, Powhatan's daughter, and held her as leverage. The move exposed the limits of Powhatan's power. Negotiations followed, and hostilities eased. When peace finally came, it was sealed not by treaty but by marriage.

On April 5, 1614, Pocahontas married John Rolfe, a rising tobacco planter whose success was reshaping the colony's future. The union was political, yet not purely coerced. Contemporary accounts suggest mutual affection, and Pocahontas had already spent years among the English, learning their language, customs, and faith. Before the wedding, she converted to Christianity and took the name Rebecca.

The marriage ushered in a fragile calm often called the Peace of Pocahontas. For several years, violence receded, trade resumed, and Jamestown stabilized. Tobacco spread relentlessly along the rivers, consuming land faster than diplomacy could restrain. Powhatan sued for peace not because he trusted the English but because the war had reached a dead end—and because his daughter's captivity had forced his hand.

The peace did not last. It could not. What Jamestown had nearly lost through starvation, it would regain through expansion. The marriage bought time, not coexistence. Powhatan understood this.

By the time Powhatan withdrew from direct contact with the English, retreating inland and allowing subordinates to manage relations, the balance had shifted. Jamestown survived. Tobacco transformed the colony's economy. English settlements multiplied along the rivers, fencing fields and redefining space in ways the Chesapeake world could not accommodate.

Pocahontas. By Simon van de Passe - National Portrait Gallery, Public Domain.

Powhatan died around 1618, as the consequences of English permanence became unmistakable. He did not live to see the full unraveling of his world, but he had seen enough to know that coexistence had failed. Leadership passed to successors who would confront the colony more directly and violently, no longer believing accommodation possible.

Powhatan

Powhatan's legacy is often reduced to his encounters with the English—to moments of ceremony, negotiation, or mythologized drama. That framing misses the point. His true achievement was not how he dealt with the newcomers but the world he had built before they arrived: a river-based political system finely tuned to the Chesapeake's rhythms. It was strong enough to absorb strangers—briefly. It was not strong enough to survive a settler empire.

The tide he mastered for a lifetime carried something upstream that, once it arrived, could not turn back. In the end, Powhatan did not lose a war. He lost a wager—that the English might be managed like any other rival.

Opechancanough

Sachem, Powhatan Confederacy

1554 – 1646

Chapter 16— Opechancanough, Powhatan Confederacy

What you do not know, you will fear. What one fears, one destroys.

—Chief Dan George

The War That Could Not Be Won

OPECHANCANOUGH UNDERSTOOD SOMETHING POWHATAN never did: that time could be a weapon, but only if it was used before it ran out.

He was already an old man when Jamestown took root along the James River, a veteran of warfare and diplomacy in a Chesapeake world that prized patience over spectacle. Opechancanough was Powhatan's brother and eventual successor, but he was never merely an inheritor. He was the confederacy's hard edge—the man entrusted with war when persuasion failed. From the outset, he distrusted English intentions.

The Jamestown settlement was not a trading post or a temporary foothold but a seed. It would grow, spread, and consume the land it touched. The marriage peace brokered through Pocahontas had slowed the advance but not its course.

Where Powhatan had ruled through accommodation— absorbing rivals, managing outsiders, and bending conflict away from destruction—Opechancanough saw the limits of restraint. He had watched the English starve and nearly disappear. He had watched them survive. From the beginning, he understood that the newcomers intended to stay.

Born around 1555, Opechancanough came of age long before the English arrived on the Chesapeake rivers. By the time he succeeded his brother as paramount leader in 1618, the land he had known had been transformed.

Opechancanough

Tobacco had reshaped Virginia into a land-hungry engine. English settlements pushed upriver and outward, fencing fields, cutting forests, and redefining land as property rather than relationship. The plant demanded land, and land demanded removal. English settlements multiplied along the navigable rivers, hardening from fragile outposts into permanent claims. Communities such as Henricus, Bermuda Hundred, Martin's Hundred, and Shirley Hundred spread outward from the James, fencing fields, clearing forests, and steadily pushing into Native space. With every ship that arrived from England, the balance shifted further out of reach.

The Powhatan world—built on rivers, tribute, and seasonal use—could not coexist with a people who never intended to stop arriving.

It was Opechancanough who captured Captain John Smith in the winter of 1607 and delivered him to Powhatan.[1] The episode, later wrapped in myth, was at its core an act of reconnaissance. Smith was questioned, assessed, and ultimately released—not because the English posed no threat, but because the nature of that threat was still unclear. Over time, that threat became unmistakable.

For years, he permitted trade and received envoys. He allowed the English to believe peace had taken hold. He watched. English settlements grew complacent, scattered across the countryside, lightly defended, and poorly coordinated.

When the moment came, Opechancanough struck with a precision that stunned the colony. On March 22, 1622,

Powhatan warriors attacked English settlements across the tidewater in a coordinated assault that unfolded within hours.

Engraving of 1622 Powhatan Massacre

The assault struck settlements on both banks of the James River—from Newport News Point near the river's mouth to Falling Creek at the fall line. Within hours, roughly a third of Virginia's English population lay dead, including more than 300 men, women, and children. Jamestown itself survived only because of a warning delivered at the last moment. The attack was not indiscriminate violence. It was strategic, aimed at erasing the colony before it could become permanent.[2]

It failed.

The English response was absolute. What followed was not war as Opechancanough understood it but extermination. Crops were burned. Villages were destroyed. Food supplies—the backbone of Powhatan survival—were deliberately targeted. The English no longer spoke of coexistence. They spoke of elimination. Hundreds of Native people were killed in the years that followed, including warriors poisoned at Jamestown during what were purportedly peace negotiations.

Opechancanough did not retreat. He adapted.

For more than two decades, he resisted English expansion through ambush, attrition, and refusal to submit. Even as his people were pushed off their lands and weakened by disease, he held the confederacy together by sheer force of will.

More than twenty years later, on April 18, 1644, he launched one last effort to expel the colonists, sparking the Third Anglo-Powhatan War. Old, blind, and reportedly carried on a litter, he struck again with devastating effect. Once again, the English survived. This time, the English finished the work.

In 1646, Opechancanough was captured, then believed to be between 90 and 100 years old. He was paraded through Jamestown before a jeering crowd, reduced from sovereign leader to spectacle.

Even in defeat, he refused to be humiliated. When guards mocked him, he fixed them with a stare witnesses described as commanding. He was shot in custody in 1646, his death unceremonious, his war unfinished.

Opechancanough leading his warriors, by Van Ingen and Snyder (via Mary Tucker Magill), Public Domain.

With Opechancanough's death, organized resistance in the Chesapeake collapsed. The treaties that followed dismantled what remained of the Powhatan world. Native peoples were confined, subordinated, and erased from Virginia's political map. Rivers became borders. Land became a commodity. The Chesapeake that Opechancanough had fought to preserve was transformed beyond recognition. What he had tried to prevent became absolute.

Opechancanough did not misunderstand the English. He understood them too well. His failure was not one of judgment, but of timing. He fought the right war—too late.

Where Powhatan had tried to manage empire, Opechancanough tried to stop it. Neither succeeded. But in the long collapse of the Chesapeake world, Opechancanough stands as its final, defiant voice—a leader who chose resistance not out of desperation, but clarity.

[1] Lemay, J. A. Leo. Did Pocahontas Save Captain John Smith? Athens, Georgia: The University of Georgia Press, 1992.
[2] Campbell, Charles (1860). History of the Colony and Ancient Dominion of Virginia. J.B. Lippincott and Company.

Closing Thoughts

What Endured, What Was Lost

The story told across these chapters is not one of inevitable collapse but of repeated choice—made under pressure, shaped by geography, and constrained by forces that tightened with each passing decade. From the rocky coasts of the Gulf of Maine to the tidal rivers of the Chesapeake, Indigenous leaders confronted the same problem in different forms: how to respond to outsiders who arrived as guests and remained as claimants.

Again and again, the land set the terms. Waterways that had once bound Native worlds together—estuaries, bays, and rivers that served as corridors of trade and diplomacy—became conduits for invasion. European ships followed the same routes canoes had traveled for generations, but they carried a different logic. Where Indigenous societies understood land as shared and seasonal, colonists reduced it to property: surveyed and fenced. What could not be reconciled was purpose.

The leaders profiled here were not naïve, passive, or uniform in their responses. Some sought accommodation, believing coexistence was possible if carefully managed. Others turned to war, understanding that delay only strengthened the settler foothold. Many tried both. None succeeded in preserving the world they had inherited. That failure was not personal. It was structural. No strategy—diplomatic, martial, or spiritual—could halt an expanding settler society fueled by population growth, capital, and imperial backing.

Yet collapse is not the same as disappearance. These nations did not vanish when treaties were broken or wars were lost. They adapted, endured, and survived—often in fragments, often under new names, often pushed west or confined to margins. The erasure came later, in memory and myth, when complexity was flattened into morality tales, and resistance was recast as savagery.

What emerges most clearly is that early American history was never a simple contest between civilization and wilderness. It was a struggle between competing systems of land use, authority, and belonging. Indigenous leaders understood the stakes early. Colonists eventually understood them. By then, the outcome had hardened.

These were not the last Native leaders to confront displacement, nor the last to resist it. But they were among the first to face a settler empire that did not intend to retreat. Their decisions—measured, defiant, tragic, and rational—shaped the continent that followed. To understand them is not to romanticize loss, but to restore agency to those who fought to remain in a world being taken from them.

Acknowledgements

This book rests on ground shaped by many hands, voices, and memories—most of them not my own. It draws first on the work of historians, archaeologists, linguists, and ethnohistorians whose careful scholarship makes it possible to reconstruct Native worlds that colonial records often distorted or ignored. I am indebted to those who read treaties skeptically, who treat oral tradition as evidence rather than embellishment, and who insist that Indigenous political systems be understood on their own terms, not through European analogies.

I am especially grateful to the Indigenous nations whose histories form the spine of this volume. While this book is written for a general audience, it is informed by generations of Native persistence—by communities who preserved language, place-names, kinship structures, and memory through removal, fragmentation, and erasure. Any clarity in these pages belongs to them. Any shortcomings are mine.

Thanks are also due to archivists and librarians, particularly those working in regional historical societies and small collections, where crucial details often survive outside the spotlight. Maps, land records, missionary accounts, court proceedings, and town histories—deeply flawed as many of them are—remain essential tools when read against the grain. This book would not exist without the patient work of those who preserve such material and make it accessible.

Finally, I owe thanks to the readers who believe that early American history still matters—not as myth, but as consequence. The past traced here is not settled. It continues to shape the present landscape, the present law, and the present reckoning with what was taken, what endured, and what was never surrendered. This volume is offered in that spirit.

Notes on Sources

This is a work of narrative history written for general readers. The goal is clarity without oversimplifying what the evidence can—and cannot—support. For many Native nations of the eastern seaboard, the documentary record is uneven by design: most surviving written sources were produced by Europeans with their own aims, blind spots, and incentives. Those accounts can be invaluable, but they must be handled like contested testimony—compared, contextualized, and read against what they leave out.

Where possible, this book leans on primary materials: treaties and land deeds; colonial correspondence; court records; missionary reports; shipping logs; town and provincial papers; and early printed narratives. These sources often preserve names, locations, and sequences of events, but they also frequently mis-hear Native languages, compress complex political systems into European categories, and treat Indigenous people as obstacles rather than governments. Throughout, I have tried to avoid presenting any single colonial observer as definitive, especially when their claims are contradicted by other records.

To balance those limitations, I relied heavily on modern scholarship to reconstruct Indigenous geographies, political relationships, and patterns of movement.

Names and spellings require special care. Tribal and community names appear in multiple forms across English, French, and Dutch records, and many were recorded phonetically. In this volume, I generally use the most widely accepted modern form for readability while acknowledging alternate spellings where they matter for identification. Geographic references use modern place names for orientation, but the underlying intent is always to point back to Indigenous homelands and watersheds, not colonial jurisdictions.

Finally, a practical note for readers: this book is not intended as a comprehensive academic catalogue of every document or interpretation. Instead, the endnotes are designed to be usable—pointing you to the best sources behind key claims and to the works that shaped the narrative most directly.

Author's Note

This book is part of Spirits Unbroken, a multi-volume series exploring Indigenous leadership across North America, organized by region. Each volume combines individual life stories with regional history to show how Native nations confronted colonization not as a single people, but as distinct societies with their own traditions of leadership, diplomacy, and survival.

The leaders featured here acted under extraordinary pressure. They faced invasion, epidemic disease, internal divisions, shifting alliances, and relentless demands for land. Their choices—to resist, negotiate, adapt, or withdraw—were shaped by circumstances few people today can fully imagine. This book does not judge those decisions by modern standards, nor does it turn these figures into symbols or legends. It presents them as people making difficult choices in real time, with limited options and lasting consequences.

The narrative draws on contemporary accounts, treaty records, colonial correspondence, and later Indigenous and historical scholarship. Where the record is incomplete or filtered primarily through European observers, those limits are acknowledged. Oral traditions are included with care and identified as such when they inform the story.

This is not a comprehensive history of every nation discussed. Instead, it seeks to restore context and agency to leaders whose lives are often reduced to brief mentions in broader colonial narratives, and to place their decisions back into the world in which they were made.

Further Reading

The works listed below are offered as pathways, reflecting the scholarship that most directly shaped this volume. They provide starting points for readers seeking to explore specific regions, nations, or themes in greater depth. Together, they balance narrative history, Indigenous-centered scholarship, archaeology, and Atlantic-world context.

<u>Foundational Works on Native America & Early Contact</u>

Facing East from Indian Country — Daniel K. Richter

A landmark reinterpretation of early American history that centers Native perspectives and political agency.

Changes in the Land — William Cronon

Essential for understanding how ecology, economy, and colonization reshaped Native and colonial worlds.

The Middle Ground — Richard White

A foundational study of diplomacy, accommodation, and power in Native–European relations.

<u>Northeast, Hudson Valley, and New England</u>

The Algonquian Peoples of the Northeast — Kathleen J. Bragdon

A clear, accessible overview of Algonquian-speaking nations, language, and culture.

Native People of Southern New England — William S. Simmons

A classic regional study grounded in anthropology and ethnohistory.

The Name of War — Jill Lepore

A deeply researched examination of King Philip's War and its lasting consequences.

The Munsee Indians — Herbert C. Kraft

Valuable for understanding Lenape regional divisions and early colonial pressure.

Haudenosaunee (Iroquois Confederacy) & Interior Power

The Ambiguous Iroquois Empire — Daniel K. Richter

A careful reassessment of Haudenosaunee power, diplomacy, and myth.

Iroquois Diplomacy on the Early American Frontier — Timothy J. Shannon

Explores how Native diplomacy shaped colonial outcomes.

Chesapeake & Mid-Atlantic Worlds

Powhatan's World and Colonial Virginia — Helen C. Rountree

The definitive study of the Powhatan Confederacy and its political system.

Pocahontas, Powhatan, Opechancanough — Helen C. Rountree

A grounded corrective to popular myths surrounding early Virginia.

Indians of the Chesapeake Bay Area — Frank W. Porter III

Useful for regional context and inter-tribal relationships.

Wabanaki & the Northeast Borderlands

The Wabanakis of Maine and the Maritimes — Harald E. L. Prins

An accessible introduction to Wabanaki history and culture.

Mi'kmaq and Maliseet Cultural History — John G. Reid

Places Wabanaki peoples within the broader Atlantic world.

Indigenous Perspectives & Modern Scholarship

Native America: A History — Colin G. Calloway

A broad, readable synthesis that keeps Indigenous experience at the center.

Why You Can't Teach United States History Without American Indians — Susan Sleeper-Smith et al.

A corrective collection emphasizing Native continuity and survival.

This list is selective by design. It reflects works most helpful for understanding Indigenous political worlds, regional dynamics, and the realities of first contact and colonization described in this volume. Readers interested in deeper archival or archaeological detail will find those paths branching outward from these titles.

Study Guide: *Echoes of the Eastern Shore*

How to Use This Book

Echoes of the Eastern Shore is not a single story but a layered one. It follows Native leaders and nations along the Atlantic seaboard as they navigated the arrival of Europeans, the rise of colonial power, and the slow transformation of their homelands into something unrecognizable. The chapters are written as narrative history, but they are intended to be read comparatively— across regions, across decades, and across different kinds of leadership.

This study guide is designed for discussion, not testing. It can be used in classrooms, book clubs, or individual reading. Questions are open-ended and thematic. Readers are encouraged to bring in additional perspectives, including contemporary Native voices, local history, and parallel events elsewhere in early America.

Core Themes of the Book

Geography as Power

Rivers, bays, coastlines, and portage routes shape nearly every decision described in this book. Control of waterways often mattered more than control of territory.

Diplomacy Before War

Native leaders repeatedly pursued negotiation, alliance, and accommodation long before resorting to violence—often with more sophistication than their colonial counterparts.

Misunderstanding and Mistranslation

Language barriers, cultural assumptions, and differing concepts of land ownership underlie many conflicts more than outright hostility.

Survival vs. Victory

For Native nations, survival often replaced victory as the primary goal. What that meant—and what it cost—varies from chapter to chapter.

Colonial Power as a Process

Colonization unfolds gradually: through trade, law, religion, and paperwork, not just warfare.

Memory and Erasure

Who is remembered, how they are named, and what survives in the historical record are recurring concerns throughout the book.

Section I: Leadership and Authority

1. How did Native leadership differ from European models of authority during the same period?

2. In what ways did sachems and chiefs derive legitimacy—from kinship, persuasion, tradition, or force?

3. Why do colonial records so often misunderstand Native titles as personal names? What does this reveal about colonial assumptions?

4. Compare two leaders in the book who made very different choices when faced with European expansion. What shaped those differences?

5. How does leadership change once war becomes unavoidable?

Section II: Diplomacy, Treaties, and Trust

1. Why were treaties such a powerful—and dangerous—tool in early America?

2. How did Native concepts of land use and shared space clash with European legal frameworks?

3. Discuss an example where a treaty appeared to promise peace but instead accelerated conflict.

4. Why did some Native leaders continue to negotiate even after repeated betrayals?

5. How does the Walking Purchase illustrate the limits of diplomacy when one side controls the legal system?

Section III: Geography and Regional Power

1. Why do rivers appear so frequently as centers of conflict and cooperation in the book?

2. Compare coastal Native communities with interior or river-valley groups. How did geography shape their exposure to Europeans?

3. How did proximity to Dutch, English, or French settlements change Native political calculations?

4. Why did some regions experience sustained resistance while others saw rapid dispossession?

5. How does the Hudson River function as both a trade corridor and a fault line?

Section IV: War and Its Consequences

1. What distinguishes King Philip's War from earlier conflicts described in the book?

2. Why was this war so destructive to Native communities compared to colonial losses?

3. How did alliances—both Native and colonial—shift during the war, and why?

4. What role did other Native nations play in determining the war's outcome?

5. In what ways did the end of the war mark not a conclusion, but a transformation?

Section V: Survival, Adaptation, and Loss

1. What strategies did Native communities use to survive after military defeat?

2. How did survival sometimes require cooperation with colonial authorities?

3. Discuss the long-term effects of displacement on Native political identity.

4. Why is survival itself framed as a form of resistance in this book?

5. How does endurance differ from sovereignty—and why does that distinction matter?

Section VI: Memory, Narrative, and History

1. Why are some Native leaders remembered primarily through colonial names and descriptions?

2. How does the absence of Native-written records shape what we think we know?

3. In what ways does modern scholarship attempt to correct earlier historical distortions?

4. Why does narrative history remain important for understanding Indigenous pasts?

5. How should readers approach uncertainty and contradiction in early American sources?

Comparative & Reflective Questions

1. Which leader in the book faced the most constrained set of choices? Why?

2. How might the story of early America change if told primarily from Native perspectives?

3. What parallels can you draw between early colonial expansion and later American history?

4. How does this book challenge familiar myths about cooperation and conflict?

5. What responsibilities do modern readers have when engaging with this history?

Optional Extension Topics

1. Compare Native diplomacy in the Northeast with that of the Southeast or Great Lakes regions.

2. Explore how modern Native nations interpret the events described in this book.

3. Examine how geography continues to influence political power today.

4. Investigate how museums, monuments, and public memory reflect—or erase—Native history.

5. Read a contemporary Native historian alongside this book and compare narrative approaches.

Closing Note

This study guide is not meant to close discussion, but to open it. The history traced in Echoes of the Eastern Shore did not end with colonial victory or Native defeat. Its consequences remain embedded in land, law, and memory. Engaging with that legacy requires patience, humility, and a willingness to sit with complexity—qualities this book invites, rather than resolves.

About the Author

Ward McLendon is a writer and analyst whose work explores the intersection of history and culture. A former public opinion analyst and message strategist, he has advised political campaigns, environmental organizations, CEOs, and philanthropic foundations on how ideas move people.

He is also the author of The Ghost Dance War and Women on the Prairie, and he recently modernized the classic A History of Kansas, updating it from its original 1919 publication, which traces the state's past from frontier settlement to statehood.

A Request from the Author

If this book spoke to you, a short book review is appreciated.

Reviews keep nonfiction history accessible to future generations and are greatly appreciated by authors and independent publishers like us.

More by Ward McLendon

The full catalog of books by Ward McLendon can be found at www.wardmclendon.com

A History of Kansas (Annotated Edition by Anna Arnold)

The Ghost Dance War
The Story of Hope, Fear, and the Road to Wounded Knee

Women on the Prairie
Stories of Grit, Survival, and Unbroken Spirit

Spirits Unbroken: *Indigenous America Series*
Last Council Fires (coming soon)
Twelve Chiefs of the Colonial Southeast

Coming Soon:

Bleeding Kansas: A Reader's Companion

Early Topeka

More Books by <u>Unbound Press</u>

Fault Lines: *Titanic Micro-histories*
<u>Steerage and Steel</u>
The True Story of Titanic's Crew and Immigrants

<u>Ladies First</u>
Titanic's Reckoning with Wealth and Worth

<u>American Silencer</u>
A History of Political Violence in America

America Uncovered
<u>Dawn of an Empire</u>
St. Augustine and The Spanish Founding of America

Women Between the Lines: *Overlooked Lives That Shaped History*

<u>Mothers, Sisters, Soldiers, Spies</u>
Women at War in American History

<u>Troublesome Women</u>
America's Whistleblowers, Cultural Pioneers, and the Women Who Changed the Rules

---

<u>Hitler's Jewish Wife</u>
The DNA of Eva Braun & The Secret of The Third Reich

Preview of the Ghost Dance War, by Ward McLendon

The following pages include a preview from The Ghost
Dance War, available at bookstores and online at
Amazon.com, Barnes and Noble, and
www.unboundpressbooks.com

THE
GHOST DANCE
WAR

A Story of Hope, Fear, and the Road to
the Massacre at Wounded Knee

WARD MCLENDON

Introduction

THE GHOST DANCE DID not begin as a rebellion. It began as a prayer.

It was delivered through visions and songs, driven by a desperate hope that the world could be restored after decades of loss. The loss of land, freedom, ceremony, and the right to live as a sovereign people. But within two years, that hope clashed with federal fear, military misjudgment, and a national desire to erase anything opposing the march of American expansion.

This book tells the story of that collision.

It traces the journey from its inception in Nevadan prophecy to its expansion across the Plains; from reservation hunger and broken treaties to Washington's panic over "uprisings" that never truly happened. It explores the political, military, tribal, and personal choices that tightened around the Lakota people like a noose. It also follows how misunderstanding turned into policy, policy into force, and force into the massacre at Wounded Knee.

This is not a retelling of Bury My Heart at Wounded Knee, but rather a focused reconstruction of the Ghost Dance era itself: the spiritual renewal, the increasing misinformation, the deadly choices, and the final moments that changed Native–U.S. relations for generations.

The aim is to show what happened, why it occurred, and how a movement rooted in peace became the pretext for the final major event of the Indian Wars.

If America wants to understand the cost of its westward triumph and the roots of its unresolved historical divides, it must understand the Ghost Dance War.

Chapter 1 — The World Before: Life on the Great Plains
and a Continent in Collapse

*"The American Indian is of the soil, whether it be the
region of forests, plains, pueblos, or mesas. He fits into the
landscape, for the hand that fashioned the continent also
fashioned the man for his surroundings. He once grew as
naturally as the wild sunflowers; he belongs just as the
buffalo belonged."*

– Luther Standing Bear, Oglala Sioux Chief

A World Unraveled

THE GREAT PLAINS, KNOWN for its vast, flat terrain, is
an expanse of grasslands in central North America,
stretching from the Rocky Mountains to the Missouri River.
Once primarily grazing territory for wild buffalo and home
to many nomadic Native American tribes, by 1890, it was
overrun by adventurers, hopeful pioneers, miners, and
missionaries.

By that time, the opening of the American West had been
unfolding for nearly 100 years.

It started in 1803 with the Louisiana Purchase, which
doubled the size of the United States and included vast
territories west of the Mississippi River. President Thomas
Jefferson negotiated the purchase of what was then known
as the Louisiana Territory from France, adding 828,000
square miles to the U.S. and significantly fueling westward
expansion.

In the years following the Louisiana Purchase, the United
States still knew very little about the vast lands it had

acquired on paper. To remedy this, President Jefferson commissioned the Lewis and Clark Corps of Discovery to explore the new territory; an expedition meant not only to map rivers and mountains but also to establish contact with the Native nations already living there.

The Corps' journals describe dozens of first encounters: diplomatic councils held along riverbanks, exchanges of gifts and food, efforts to establish trade, and cautious introductions between worlds that had never met on equal footing. Lewis and Clark arrived with instructions to present the United States as the new sovereign power, yet most tribes viewed the expedition as just another group of travelers passing through their homelands.

The expedition's notes showcase the vast diversity of Native societies across the West. They documented established trade routes, intertribal alliances, complex political structures, thriving economies, and legal and ceremonial systems that predate the United States. Many communities were flourishing, mobile, and, despite disruptions from earlier European contact, still deeply connected to their traditional ways.

But the Corps of Discovery was also a hinge moment.

It marked the first sustained encounter between the U.S. federal government and the Western tribes, and, in retrospect, the start of a century-long clash. The expedition's maps opened the West to American settlement; its reports fueled land speculation; its diplomatic overtures signaled future claims of authority. What Lewis and Clark saw as exploration, later policymakers regarded as justification.

The West was no longer an unfamiliar land. It was a territory the United States now intended to occupy.

Westward Push

During the 1840s and 1850s, the idea of "Manifest Destiny" drove further expansion, with key events such as the annexation of Texas in 1845, the Oregon Treaty of 1846, and the Mexican Cession in 1848, which added vast lands in the Southwest. Waves of settlers, miners, railroad workers, ranchers, and homesteaders moved west as the government promoted free land. Described as "unused" and available, federal land grants supported railroad construction, and the Homestead Act opened millions of acres for pioneer claims.

Across the plains, this change arrived in waves. Wagon by wagon, ranch by ranch, mining camp by mining camp. As pioneers pushed westward, the United States turned Native homelands into barriers to clear or control. When settlers moved further into Indigenous lands, the government responded not by halting the expansion but by restructuring Native nations, removing communities, redrawing boundaries, and deploying troops to secure the new frontier for American migration.

The Homestead Act of 1862 further encouraged settlers to claim land in areas the Lakota and other Plains tribes had relied on for generations. Each wagon trail crossing the plains undermined tribal sovereignty. Every new mining camp brought another intrusion. As pioneers moved westward, federal policies shifted to support the influx of settlers rather than those already living there.

By the 1870s and 1880s, U.S. policy had aligned around a single goal: to dismantle Native American independence and foster dependency. Resistance by tribes was met with military enforcement. Buffalo herds, once numbering in the tens of millions, were deliberately and systematically slaughtered to clear land for railroads and ranches. Federal Indian agents managed food distribution, withheld supplies as punishment, and enforced a new political order. The change was not just territorial; it marked a shift from sovereignty to surveillance, from nation to ward.

By 1887, mining, industrial expansion, and large-scale migration were reshaping the land, with cities and towns sprouting across the landscape and the rush for land and resources continuing strong. Railroad development cut through migration routes and hunting grounds.

The West was no longer a frontier of the past but a dynamic, rapidly changing part of the nation.

In this churn of movement and ambition, the Lakota stood at the center of the storm. To them, and other native inhabitants of the West, it seemed that a way of life that had lasted for generations was ending.

The Dawes Act

The Dawes Act of 1887, also known as the General Allotment Act, was a U.S. law that allowed the federal government to divide tribal lands into individual plots to encourage assimilation. It divided tribal communal land

and assigned 160 acres to each Native American family, in the mistaken hope that they would become farmers.

It resulted in the loss of over 90 million acres of native land.

The goal, of course, was to assimilate Native Americans by ending their communal land ownership and encouraging them to adopt private property and farming, believing this would "civilize" them. What they truly wanted was for them to disappear. By breaking up the tribal structure of the indigenous nations, the government was sending a message: You're no longer part of a tribe; you are individual landowners; you are Americans.

Only those Native Americans who accepted individual allotments were granted U.S. citizenship. The remaining "surplus" tribal lands were then sold to non-Native settlers and corporations.

The Dawes Act, a well-meaning effort to help Indians, ended up hurting them instead. By 1890, no Indian people lived freely on their own land.

The Lakota

Before this expansion, the Lakota occupied one of the largest Indigenous territories in North America. Their land extended from the western banks of the Missouri River to the Powder River area in what is now Wyoming and Montana, and south into the Sandhills and Niobrara region of Nebraska. This landscape was not empty; it was full of meaning, memory, and movement.

The Lakota were one of the three main divisions of the Sioux Nation, along with Dakota and Nakota, forming the westernmost and most mobile branch. They had called the Plains home for over a century, and the sacred center of their world was the Black Hills (Pahá Sápa).

The Lakota were not simply residents of the land; they were its stewards. Over generations, they developed a network of trade, diplomacy, and seasonal migrations that connected them deeply to the rhythms of rivers, plains, and the sacred Black Hills. They were neither isolated nor static. Their influence stretched through alliances with tribes like the Cheyenne and Arapaho and through conflicts with the Crow, Pawnee, and others. They were a nation in the truest sense: sovereign, adaptable, interconnected, and mobile.

By the early 19th century, they had expanded westward after gaining horses and firearms and developing a culture well-suited to the grasslands.

Lakota society was organized around extended families, or tiyospaye, which formed the core of social and political life. Decisions were made through consensus, not command; leaders earned influence through generosity, skill, and moral authority rather than inherited or coercive power. The political structure was decentralized yet cohesive, allowing bands to act independently but unite against common threats.

White explorers who encountered them in the 1830s and 1840s repeatedly remarked on their population, their political cohesion, and the strength of their military organization. These were not fragmented or vulnerable people. This was a nation at its height.

Their society was finely adapted to the world around them: mobile, resilient, bound by kin groups, and organized through a decentralized but cohesive political structure.

They maintained extensive trade networks stretching from the Upper Mississippi to the foothills of the Rockies; governed themselves through a combination of band councils, respected leaders, and consensus decision-making; and upheld a social order that balanced personal freedom with communal responsibility.

Their life revolved around mobility, seasonal migration, and the buffalo, which provided food, clothing, shelter, tools, and spiritual grounding. To the Lakota, the land was not a possession but a living system: one they belonged to, moved through, and protected.

Their mobility was strategic, not improvised: the seasonal hunting routes, winter camps along sheltered river valleys, and intertribal diplomacy that managed alliances, marriages, and conflicts across a broad area created a stable political and cultural system. This system was adaptable enough to shift with the seasons while remaining strong enough to maintain unity among the people.

Spiritually, the Lakota saw the world as animated by interconnected forces, with wakan, the sacred power that flowed through everything at its center. Ceremonies such as the Sun Dance, sweat lodge, and vision quests tied individuals to the community and the cosmos. Their culture had resilience and balance precisely because it was oriented toward relational, not hierarchical, principles. These vision quests and ceremonies were not peripheral to life; they were integral to how the Lakota were bonded to one another, to the land, and to their ancestors.

This was the world that collided with U.S. expansion. A society built on mobility confronted a policy built on confinement. A political order grounded in consensus met a federal system that insisted on singular, enforceable authority. A people whose identity was rooted in the land found themselves pushed off it, parcel by parcel.

The Buffalo

The buffalo, which had been central to the economic, spiritual, and social life of Plains nations for decades, was the first great foundation to fall. In the early 1800s, tens of millions roamed the Plains. By 1889, fewer than a thousand remained in the wild.

The loss was fueled by commercial hide-hunting industries that exploded after 1870, fueled by new tanning technologies, aggressive railroad promotions, and a tacit military belief that buffalo eradication would force Native populations into dependency. Without the buffalo, tribal autonomy collapsed.

The Spark at Bozeman

The tension between tribes and the U.S. government grew worse in the 1860s when the Army opened the Bozeman Trail, a shortcut heading north into the Montana goldfields that cut straight through hunting grounds guaranteed to the Lakota by the 1851 treaty. The Powder River country, home to some of the last great buffalo herds, was not just a resource base; it was a cultural heartland, a place where generations of Lakota hunted, fought, negotiated, and prayed.

Red Cloud, a prominent Oglala war chief, immediately realized that the trail threatened not just mobility but their very survival. The Army started building forts to guard the road, and Red Cloud viewed each fort as a blow to Lakota sovereignty.

He responded with resistance rather than with diplomacy.

Between 1866 and 1868, Red Cloud led a coalition of Lakota, Cheyenne, and Arapaho warriors in what became known as Red Cloud's War. Through strategic ambushes, raids, and a deep understanding of the terrain, he achieved something rare in U.S.-Native conflict history: he forced the United States Army to retreat.

In 1868, the U.S. abandoned the forts and closed the Bozeman Trail. The victory was complete, but the repercussions would endure.

Fort Laramie and the Shifting Promises of a Nation

By the time Ulysses S. Grant took office in 1869, the United States was facing increasing conflicts with Native Americans across the West.

Grant's "Peace Policy," which aimed to reduce frontier violence and corruption, delegated control of many reservations to Christian denominations. Agents appointed under this system were often chosen based on religious ties rather than cultural understanding. They pushed for rapid assimilation, promoted English-only schools, banned ceremonies, and tried to restructure Native governance.

The paternalism of this policy sharply conflicted with the Lakota's political worldview. Leaders like Red Cloud, Spotted Tail, and Crazy Horse were used to negotiating from positions of strength. Now they had to contend with civilian agents who neither understood nor respected Lakota authority.

Tensions grew. Accusations of ration withholding, disrespect, and coercion became common. Several agents worked honestly and with some sympathy, but many others viewed Lakota culture as a problem to be corrected.

For the Lakota, the Peace Policy felt very much like a war on their identity. It attempted to remake them without their consent. And it prepared the ground for conflicts that would erupt in the mid-1870s.

Among the most important agreements between the Lakota and the U.S. government was the 1868 Fort Laramie Treaty, signed after years of fighting along the Bozeman Trail. It granted the Lakota ownership of the Black Hills (Pahá Sápa) and a large territory set aside for their use. It also assured hunting rights, schools, rations, agency buildings, and protection from the Army against settlers moving in. For a time, it seemed to provide a stable peace.

That illusion lasted less than a decade.

To continue reading The Ghost Dance War, visit www.unboundpressbooks.com or any retailer or online bookstore.

250